NELL: An SVG Drawing Language

Stefan Hollos and J. Richard Hollos

NELL: An SVG Drawing Language
by Stefan Hollos and J. Richard Hollos

Abrazol Publishing
an imprint of Exstrom Laboratories LLC
662 Nelson Park Drive, Longmont, CO 80503-7674 U.S.A.

Publisher's Cataloging in Publication Data
Hollos, Stefan
NELL: An SVG Drawing Language / by Stefan Hollos and J. Richard Hollos
p. cm.
ISBN: 978-1-887187-40-4
Library of Congress Control Number: 2020932538
1. Computer graphics 2. SVG (Document markup language) 3. Programming languages (Electronic computers)
I. Title. II. Hollos, Stefan.
T385 .H65567 2020
N7433.8 .H65567 2020
006.66 HOL

About the Cover: Images created with NELL.

Contents

INTRODUCTION

Nell is a language for describing two dimensional vector drawings. We have been using versions of the language for several years to create illustrations for books, web pages and various art projects. It can even be used as a tool for physics and math simulations and experiments. You can for instance do optics ray tracing with it. There are a couple of examples later in the documentation that show how to do this.

We created the language because of our frustration with how tedious and time consuming it can be to create complex vector drawings. Why sit in front of a screen for hours clicking and dragging with a mouse when you can spend a few minutes thinking about your drawing, solving a few geometry and trigonometry problems and then writing a simple program that will create the drawing for you. It's less tedious and a lot more fun, plus you get to sharpen your math and programming skills.

A big advantage of using Nell is that you can parameterize the drawing. Lengths, angles, numbers of polygons, circles, ellipses, arcs, and curves can all be parameterized so you can easily experiment with different values and quickly see how the drawing changes. Another advantage is the simplicity of the language itself. It's so simple that it's easy to write programs that create Nell programs. We have used this technique to explore domains of possible drawings and have created thousands of interesting patterns in the process.

We usually use Nell to create just the basic outline of a complex drawing. Then if we want to decorate the drawing with different colors and line styles we use an interactive vector drawing program such as Inkscape. This is because there is currently no way to set stroke width and color for individual elements of a drawing or to set the fill color for individual polygons, circles and ellipses. We have thought about adding colors and

1

styles to Nell but have decided against it to keep the language as simple as possible. Would you like to see colors and styles in the Nell language? Let us know what you think.

To understand how to use Nell it is helpful to be at least vaguely familiar with the rudiments of Cartesian or analytic geometry. This is geometry in which points, lines and curves are defined in a coordinate system. Coordinates are sets of numbers that are used to locate the position of a point in the coordinate system. Equations are often used to relate coordinates thus defining a set of points that make up a curve. Just the basics of high school algebra and geometry is all you need to use Nell. To be a power user you probably also need to know a little basic trigonometry.

Drawings in Nell are defined in a standard two dimensional Cartesian space where the positive x axis is to the right, the positive y axis is up and a point is represented by a pair of numbers (x, y). To keep things simple it is assumed that the final drawing will always be entirely in the positive first quadrant where x and y are greater than or equal to zero. Lines and curves can extend into quadrants with negative values for x and y but the final drawing, produced as an svg file, will always be clipped to the positive first quadrant.

Drawings by default start at the origin $(0,0)$. The current position can easily be changed with the position command $P(x, y)$. At each step during the execution of a drawing there is a current position and a current direction. The direction is an angle measured relative to the positive x axis. A drawing always starts out with direction along the positive x axis i.e. at angle 0. Positive angles are measured counterclockwise and negative angles are measured clockwise. Imagine yourself facing in the current direction. A command to turn by a positive angle then means a turn to your left and a negative angle means a turn to the right.

The current position and direction are changed when drawing and positioning commands are executed. For example the command L(1) will draw a line of length 1 in the current direction starting at the current position. The new current position is at the end of the line while the current direction is unchanged. The command T(a) will turn by an angle a with respect to the current direction and make the new direction the current direction. There are other commands that change the current position and direction. You can read about them in the command definitions and example sections that follow.

Creating a drawing is a two step process. First the command line program nell reads a drawing definition file that contains variable definition lines and named command strings that are used to create the drawing. Using the defined variables, the command strings are expanded out into one long string of primitive drawing commands that is written to standard output i.e. the terminal.

The string of primitive drawing commands is read by another command line program called nellsvg. This converts the drawing commands into an svg (scalable vector graphics) file which is also written to standard output. This two step process is used so that in the future it will be easier to produce output in other file formats such as pdf with a nellpdf program for example.

The nell program takes three command line parameters and is run as follows.

```
Usage: nell ddfile scs mrl
  ddfile = name of drawing definition file.
  scs = name of starting command string.
  mrl = maximum recursion level.
```

The parameter ddfile is the name of the drawing definition file. The name can be any valid filename but for all the example drawings in this documentation we use the file extension `nll`. The parameter `scs` is the name of the starting command string, see the description of the drawing definition file and the examples that follow for an explanation of this parameter. A named command string can substitute itself and this recursion must be stopped at some point. The parameter `mrl` sets the maximum recursion level.

The `nellsvg` program takes five command line parameters and is run as follows.

```
Usage: nellsvg width height units sw fh\n", argv[0]);
  width = width of canvas.
  height = height of canvas.
  units = px pt pc cm mm in.
  sw = stroke width in given units.
  fh = 1 to flip about the horizontal.
```

The parameters `width` and `height` specify the width and height of the svg drawing. The parameter `units` gives the units of the width and height. The parameter `sw` gives the stroke width for all elements of the drawing. The parameter `fh` specifies if the drawing is to be flipped with respect to the horizontal. For `fh=1` the drawing is executed with positive y going up and positive x going right. Otherwise positive y is in the downward direction as it is in svg drawings by default.

Both the `nell` and `nellsvg` programs are written in standard C. They do not require any additional software libraries and are platform independent i.e. you should be able to compile and run them on any computer running any operating system (e.g. Linux, macOS, Windows) that has a C compiler. The programs are free open source software released under the GPL license. You can download the source code from the book's website at http://www.abrazol.com/books/nell/ and compile the programs with any C compiler. There are many programs you can use to view the svg files ranging from a web browser like Firefox to the **display** program that comes with ImageMagick.

The following is a list of source code files needed to compile the `nell` and `nellsvg` programs.

- `calcfun.h`

- `calcfun.c`

- `nell.c`

- `nellsvg.c`

If you're using the gcc compiler you can compile the two programs with the following commands.

```
gcc -lm -o nell calcfun.c nell.c
gcc -lm -o nellsvg nellsvg.c
```

Next we will describe the drawing definition file. This will be followed by many examples that show how to use the language.

In case you're wondering, the language is named after both Sister Plautilla Nelli (1524-1588), the first known female Renaissance painter of Florence, and the ladybug, which belongs to the family of small beetles called Coccinellidae.

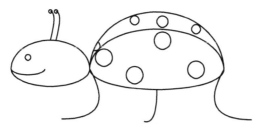

See Gallery for Nell code to draw this ladybug.

DRAWING DEFINITION FILE

A drawing definition file consists of a sequence of variable definition lines followed by lines with named command strings. It is possible to mix the order of variable definitions and command strings but it helps with readability to put all variable definitions first.

The exact syntax of these lines is defined below but common to both the variable definitions and command strings is the fact that they must both end in a semicolon. Anything after the semicolon is ignored and can be used as comments.

A line beginning with a semicolon is ignored and can be used as a comment line. Any line that does not contain a semicolon is also ignored. If a drawing fails to execute properly check that all variable definitions and command strings end in a semicolon otherwise they are ignored.

Note that the names of all variables, functions and commands are case sensitive. In other words, the variable x is different than the variable X.

Variable Definition Lines

A variable definition line takes the form of a variable name followed by an equal sign followed by a mathematical formula ending with a semicolon. There can be only one variable definition per line.

The variable name can be any alphanumeric string that does not contain whitespace. The mathematical formula can be any standard mathematical expression involving the operators +, -, *, /, ˆ (exponentiation), (,), and the functions:

sqrt(x)
Returns the positive square root of x. x must be a positive real number.

cos(x)
Returns the cosine of x which will be in the range -1 to +1. x must be in radians. To convert from degrees to radians multiply by `pi/180`.

sin(x)
Returns the sine of x which will be in the range -1 to +1. x must be in radians. To convert from degrees to radians multiply by `pi/180`.

tan(x)
Returns the tangent of x. x must be in radians. To convert from degrees to radians multiply by pi/180. Note that `tan(x)` goes to infinity as `x` approaches an odd integer multiple of `pi/2`.

acos(x)
Returns the arc cosine of x in units of radians. This is the angle whose cosine is x. The value returned will be in the range 0 to pi.

asin(x)
Returns the arc sine of x in units of radians. This is the angle whose sine is x. The value returned will be in the range -pi/2 to pi/2.

atan(x)
Returns the arc tangent of x in units of radians. This is the angle whose tangent is x. The value returned will be in the range -pi/2 to pi/2.

angle(x,y,z)
For a triangle with sides of length x, y, z, this returns the angle common to the sides of length x and y. The angle is in units of radians.

exp(x)
Returns the base of the natural logarithm raised to the power of x.

log(x)

Returns the natural logarithm of x. To find the logarithm with respect to the base b divide the result by `log(b)`.

A mathematical expression can contain previously defined variables. The variable `pi=3.14159265359` is always predefined. Arguments and return values for all trigonometric functions are in terms of radians where `pi` radians is equal to 180°.

Named Command Strings

A named command string takes the form of a name followed by a colon followed by a string of commands ending in a semicolon. The name can be any alphanumeric string that does not contain whitespace. Commands may or may not be separated by white space. To enhance readability at least one blank space should be placed between commands but it is not strictly necessary. Names are used in the substitution command defined below. It can also be used to specify the starting string of drawing commands by passing it to the `nell` program as a parameter.

The following is a list of the possible commands that may appear in a command string. Examples of how to use these commands are given in the following chapters.

L(l)

Draws a straight line of length l in the current direction starting at the current position. After this command the current position is updated to the point at the end of the line. The current direction is not changed.

Q(l,lc,ac)

Draws a quadratic Bezier curve that connects to a point a distance l in the current direction from the current position. The direction of the control point is at angle `ac` from the current direction. For `ac> 0` this is to the left of the current direction (counterclockwise) and for `ac< 0` it is to the right (clockwise). `lc` is the distance of the control point from the current point. After this command the current position is updated to the point at the end of the curve. The current direction is not changed.

B(l,lc1,ac1,lc2,ac2)

Draws a cubic Bezier curve that connects to a point a distance `l` in the current direction from the current position. `lc1` is the distance of the first control point from the start of the curve. `lc2` is the distance of the second control point from the end of the curve. `ac1` is the direction of the first control point measured with respect to the current direction at the start of the curve. `ac2` is the direction of the second control point measured with respect to the current direction at the end of the curve. For both directions, positive values are to the left and negative values are to the right of the current direction. After this command the current position is updated to the point at the end of the curve. The current direction is not changed.

C(r)

Draws a circle of radius `r` centered at the current position. Neither the current position or direction are changed. A circle cannot be part of a path.

E(rx,ry)

Draws an ellipse centered at the current position. The x and y radii of the ellipse are given by `rx` and `ry`. The ellipse is rotated so that the x-axis is in the current direction. Neither the current position or direction are changed. An ellipse cannot be part of a path.

R(rx,ry,a,da)

Draws an arc of an ellipse centered at the current position. The x and y radii of the ellipse are given by `rx` and `ry`. The ellipse is rotated so that the x-axis is in the current direction. The starting point of the arc is at angle a from the current direction. For a$>$ 0 this is to the left of the current direction (counterclockwise) and for a$<$ 0 it is to the right (clockwise). The angle swept out by the arc from the starting to the ending point is da. For da$>$ 0 the arc from start to end goes counterclockwise around the ellipse and for da$<$ 0 it goes clockwise. Neither the current position or direction are changed. An elliptic arc cannot be part of a path.

M(l)
Moves a distance l in the current direction from the current point. After this command the current position is updated to the new point. The current direction is not changed.

T(da)
Changes the current direction by the angle da. For da$>$ 0 the new direction is counterclockwise from the current direction and for da$<$ 0 it is clockwise. The current position is not changed.

P(x,y)
Sets the current position to the point (x,y). The current direction is not changed.

D(a)
Sets the current direction to the angle a. The current position is not changed.

Z()
Draws a line from the current position to the position at the start of the current path. The current position and direction are updated to the values at the start of the current path. The most common use of this command is at the end of a path just before the > symbol that closes the path but it can be appear anywhere inside a path and can appear more than once. The command takes no arguments.

<

This symbol marks the start of a new path. The current position and direction are used as the starting point of the path so they should be set to the desired values prior to starting the path. Paths cannot be nested so it is an error to use this symbol inside a currently open path.

>

This symbol marks the end of a path. It is an error to use this symbol if there is no currently open path. The current position and direction remain unchanged.

[

Saves the current position and direction. This can be nested up to 64 times.

]

Restores the most recently saved position and direction.

S(C,n)

Substitutes the command string labeled C n times. A command string can substitute itself recursively. The recursion stops when the maximum recursion level is reached. This level is specified on the command line.

A(var,exp)

Sets the variable var to the value of expression. var can be any previously defined variable or a new variable. exp can be any mathematical expression as described in the section on variable definitions.

POLYGONS

One of the simplest things you can draw is a polygon. There are many ways to draw them in Nell. To draw an equilateral triangle with sides of length 1 you could use the program (poly00.nll).

Program (poly00.nll)

```
START : L(1) T(2*pi/3) L(1) T(2*pi/3) L(1) T(2*pi/3);
```

Command line

```
nell poly00.nll START 6 | nellsvg 1 1 in 0.02 1 > poly00.svg
```

The exterior angles of an equilateral triangle are all equal to $120° = 2\pi/3$ radians, hence the T(2*pi/3) commands. The last T(2*pi/3) command is strictly not necessary. It just returns the direction to where it was at the beginning.

The program (poly00.nll) will produce an svg where each line is a separate path. To group all the lines into a single path, we simply put angle brackets around the command string as shown in program (poly00a.nll)

Program (poly00a.nll)

```
START : <L(1) T(2*pi/3) L(1) T(2*pi/3) L(1) T(2*pi/3)>;
```

Command line

```
nell poly00a.nll START 6 | nellsvg 1 1 in 0.02 1 > poly00a.svg
```

This produces an svg where the triangle is a single path, but the path is still open, i.e. the first point is not connected to the last point. A triangle that is a single closed path is produced by program (`poly01.nll`)

Program (`poly01.nll`)

```
START : <L(1) T(2*pi/3) L(1) T(2*pi/3) Z()>;
```

Command line

```
nell poly01.nll START 6 | nellsvg 1 1 in 0.02 1 > poly01.svg
```

Note that the last `L(1)` command has been left out since it is implicit in the `Z()` command which closes the path and sets the current position and direction to what it was at the start of the path.

You can use this same technique for drawing regular polygons with any number of sides, but instead of writing out the L command for each side explicitly, you can use a substitution command. The program (`poly02.nll`) shows how to do this to draw a pentagon.

Program (`poly02.nll`)

```
SIDE : L(1) T(2*pi/5);
START : M(0.5) <S(SIDE,4) Z()>;
```

Command line

```
nell poly02.nll START 6 | nellsvg 2 2 in 0.02 1 > poly02.svg
```

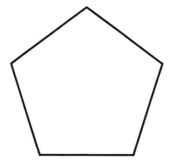

The command string labeled SIDE draws one side of the pentagon, and we use it four times inside the path to draw four sides of the polygon with the final Z command completing the last side. The initial M(0.5) command starts the drawing at the point $(0.5, 0)$ so that the entire pentagon is in the positive first quadrant.

With a substitution command and a variable definition we can easily generalize this to a program that will draw a polygon with n sides. Program (poly03.nll) shows how it's done.

Program (poly03.nll)

```
n = 6;
SIDE : L(1) T(2*pi/n);
START : M(0.5) <S(SIDE,n-1) Z()>
```

Command line
```
nell poly03.nll START 6 | nellsvg 2 2 in 0.02 1 > poly03.svg
```

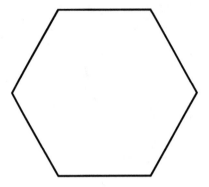

In (`poly03.nll`) we've defined the variable **n** which is set equal to 6 at the beginning of the program. If you run the program like this it will produce a hexagon. Set **n** = 8; and it will produce an octagon and so on.

So much for drawing single regular polygons. Now let's see how easy it is to create drawings with multiple polygons. You can easily make a series of nested regular polygons using a double set of substitutions. Program (`poly04.nll`) shows how it's done.

Program (`poly04.nll`)

```
n=3;
SIDE : L(1) T(2*pi/n);
POLY : <S(SIDE,n-1) Z()> A(n,n+1);
START : M(1) S(POLY,6);
```

Command line

```
nell poly04.nll START 6 | nellsvg 3 3 in 0.02 1 > poly04.svg
```

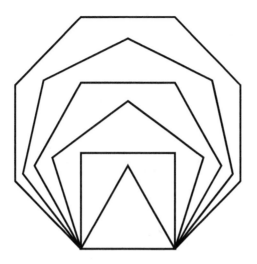

In (`poly04.nll`) we've used the `A` command that assigns a new value to a variable, which in this case is the number of sides in the next polygon to draw. The `POLY` command string is substituted 6 times with the value of `n` incremented each time, starting with the value 3. The result is that a triangle, square, pentagon, hexagon, heptagon, and octagon are drawn, all starting at the same point and sharing a common side. The `M(1)` command sets the starting point for all polygons to $(1,0)$ so they are horizontally centered on a 3×3 canvas.

Program (`poly05.nll`) shows how to arrange five pentagons so that they form a pentagon.

Program (poly05.nll)

```
SIDE : L(1) T(-2*pi/5);
POLY : <S(SIDE,4) Z()> M(1) T(2*pi/5);
START : P(2,2) S(POLY,5);
```

Command line
```
nell poly05.nll START 6 | nellsvg 5 5 in 0.02 1 > poly05.svg
```

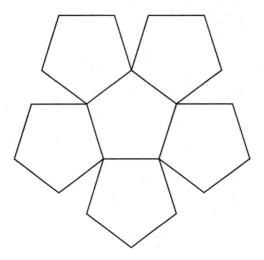

Here we've used the P command to position the starting point at $(2, 2)$. This centers the drawing on a 5×5 canvas. The POLY command string draws a pentagon, moves one unit in the current direction and changes direction by 2*pi/5 so that the next pentagon can be drawn.

The program (poly06.nll) draws a pentagram inside a pentagon.

Program (poly06.nll) Note that lines labeled PENTAGON and PENTAGRAM are broken here but are one line each in the actual file.

```
d = (1+sqrt(5))/2;
PENTAGON : <L(1) T(2*pi/5) L(1) T(2*pi/5) L(1) T(2*pi/5) L(1)
          T(2*pi/5) Z()>;
PENTAGRAM : T(pi/5) <L(d) T(4*pi/5) L(d) T(4*pi/5) L(d) T(4*pi/5)
          L(d) T(4*pi/5) Z()>;
START : M(0.5) S(PENTAGON,1) S(PENTAGRAM,1);
```

Command line
```
nell poly06.nll START 6 | nellsvg 2 2 in 0.02 1 > poly06.svg
```

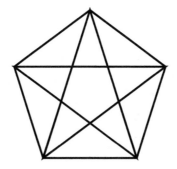

The program (`poly07.nll`) draws concentric triangles starting with the outer triangle and going in.

Program (poly07.nll)

```
n = 6;
l = 2;
dl = l/n;
dr = dl/sqrt(3);
a = 2*pi/3;
TRI : <L(l) T(a) L(l) T(a) Z()> T(pi/6) M(dr) T(-pi/6) A(l,l-dl);
START : S(TRI,n);
```

Command line
```
nell poly07.nll START 6 | nellsvg 2 2 in 0.02 1 > poly07.svg
```

The variable n defines the number of triangles to draw. The variable l is the length of a side of the outer triangle. The variable dl is the amount by which the length of the triangle side changes as you go in. The variable dr is the length by which you move in to draw the next triangle. As an exercise see if you can modify the program so the inner triangle is drawn first and the outer last.

You can generalize (poly07.nll) to draw concentric polygons with any number of sides. The program (conpoly.nll): shows how to do it.

Program (conpoly.nll)

```
ns=6;  number of sides
n=12;  number of polygons
l=2;  length of a side
dl=l/n;
dr=dl/(2*sin(pi/ns));
a=2*pi/ns;
b=pi*(ns-2)/(2*ns);
SIDE : L(l) T(a);
POLY : <S(SIDE,ns-1) Z()> T(b) M(dr) T(-b) A(l,l-dl);
START : M(l) S(POLY,n);
```

Command line
```
nell conpoly.nll START 10 | nellsvg 4 4 in 0.02 1 > conpoly.svg
```

The program defines the variable **ns** that specifies the number of sides for the polygons and the variable **b** which is the angle to turn to move to the beginning of the next inner polygon.

A variation on the concentric polygons is to rotate each of the inner polygons by half the exterior angle. The program (**rconpoly.nll**) shows how to do it.

Program (rconpoly.nll)

```
ns=8;  number of sides
```

```
n=28;   number of polygons
l=2;    length of a side
a=2*pi/ns;
rl = cos(a/2);
SIDE : L(l) T(a);
POLY : <S(SIDE,ns-1) Z()> M(l/2) T(a/2) A(1,1*rl);
START : M(sqrt(2)) S(POLY,n);
```

Command line
```
nell rconpoly.nll START 10 | nellsvg 4.83 4.83 in 0.02 1 > rconpoly.svg
```

We can also easily tile polygons. The program (`tritile.nll`) will create a tiling using triangles.

Program (`tritile.nll`)

```
n = 8;
l = 0.5;
r = 1.0;
d = r*l;
a = 2*pi/3;
T1 : <L(l) T(a) L(l) T(a) Z()> M(d);
T2 : [S(T1,n)] T(a/2) M(d) T(-a/2) [S(T1,n-1)];
T3 : [S(T2,1)] T(pi/2) M(d*sqrt(3)) T(-pi/2);
START : S(T3,n/2);
```

Command line
```
nell tritile.nll START 10 | nellsvg 4 4 in 0.02 1 > tritile.svg
```

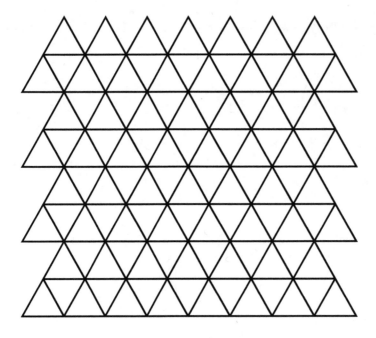

The variable n is the number of triangles per row, l is the length of a triangle side and r determines the tile spacing where r= 1 gives an exact fit, r< 1 gives an overlap, and r> 1 adds space between the triangles. For r= 1.25 we get this:

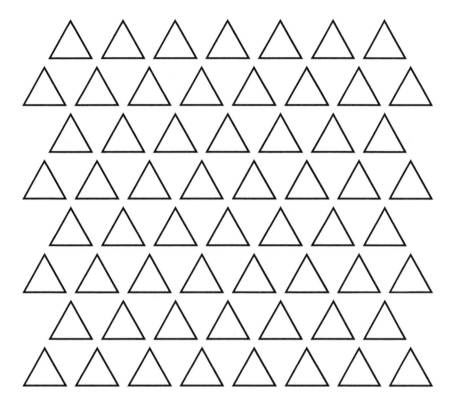

The program (`hextile.nll`) will create a tiling using hexagons.

Program (`hextile.nll`)

```
a = pi/3;
s = 0.5;
r = 1.0;
d = r*s*sqrt(3);
n = 4;
T1 : L(s) T(a);
T2 : <S(T1,5) Z()>;
T3 : S(T2,1) T(a/2) M(d) T(-a/2) S(T2,1) T(-a/2) M(d) T(a/2);
```

```
T4 : [S(T3,n)] T(pi/2) M(d) T(-pi/2);
START : M(0.25) S(T4,n);
```

Command line
```
nell hextile.nll START 10 | nellsvg 6.25 4.0 in 0.02 1 > hextile.svg
```

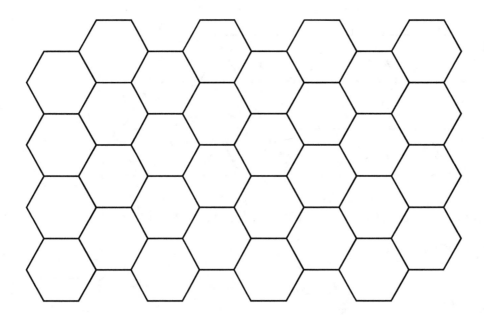

Again the variable r determines the spacing. For r= 1 there is no space between the hexagons. For r= 0.5 the hexagons overlap as in the following figure.

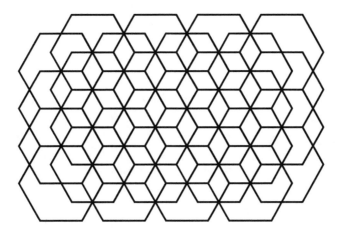

CIRCLES

You can draw a circle with the command C(r). This will draw a circle of radius r centered on the current position. The current position and direction are not changed so you can easily draw concentric circles as shown in program (circ1.nll).

Program (circ1.nll)

```
n = 10;
r = 1;
dr = 0.1;
T1 : C(r) A(r,r+dr);
START : P(2,2) S(T1,n);
```

Command line
```
nell circ1.nll START 3 | nellsvg 4 4 in 0.02 1 > circ1.svg
```

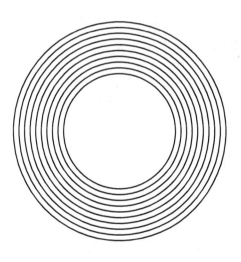

You can create a Moire pattern with two sets of equally spaced concentric circles. As you move apart the centers of the two sets of circles you will see different patterns emerge. These patterns are analogous the constructive and destructive interference produced by two point sources of light (or any source of transverse waves). Program (circ2.nll) draws two sets of 40 concentric circles spaced a distance dr = 0.05 apart with the centers of the two sets separated by a distance 4*dr = 0.2.

Program (circ2.nll)

```
n = 40;
r = 0.05;
dr = 0.05;
T1 : C(r) A(r,r+dr);
START : P(2.05,2.05) S(T1,n) A(r,dr) M(4*dr) S(T1,n)
```

Command line
```
nell circ2.nll START 3 | nellsvg 4.3 4.1 in 0.02 1 > circ2.svg
```

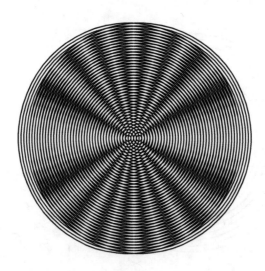

The program (`circ3.nll`) will draw a circle of radius r0 that is completely encircled by n circles. The radius of the outer circles shrinks as n increases as long as the radius of the inner circle stays constant. The square canvas size is `2*r0*(1+2*cos(b)/(1-cos(b)))` where `b=pi*(n-2)/(2*n)`.

Program (`circ3.nll`)

```
r0 = 1;
n = 12;
b = pi*(n-2)/(2*n);
x = r0/(1-cos(b)); distance from center of inner circle
r = x*cos(b); radius of outer circles
a = 2*pi/n;
T1 : [M(x) C(r)] T(a);
START : P(r0+2*r,r0+2*r) C(r0) T(-pi/2) S(T1,n);
```

Command line
```
nell circ3.nll START 10 | nellsvg 3.4 3.4 in 0.02 1 > circ3.svg
```

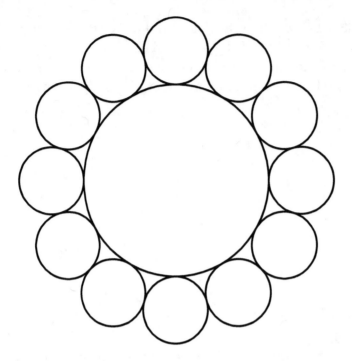

The program (`circ4.nll`) will inscribe a circle inside an n-sided regular polygon. A program for circumscribing a circle around an n-sided regular polygon would be almost identical. See if you can modify (`circ4.nll`) to circumscribe a circle. Hint the radius of the circumscribed circle is r=1/(2*cos(b)).

Program (`circ4.nll`)

```
n = 5;
l = 1;
b = pi*(n-2)/(2*n);
r = l*tan(b)/2; radius of circle
a = 2*pi/n;
T1 : L(l) T(a);
```

```
START : M(0.5) <S(T1,n-1) Z()> T(b) M(1/(2*cos(b))) C(r);
```

Command line
```
nell circ4.nll START 10 | nellsvg 2 1.6 in 0.02 1 > circ4.svg
```

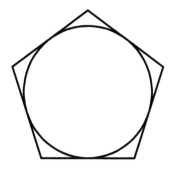

```
START : M(0.5) <S(T1,n-1) Z()> T(b) M(1/(2*cos(b))) C(r);
```

Command line
```
nell circ4.nll START 10 | nellsvg 2 1.6 in 0.02 1 > circ4.svg
```

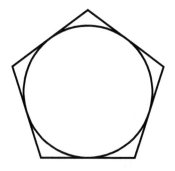

ELLIPSES

You can draw an ellipse with the command E(rx,ry) where rx is the radius of the ellipse in the current direction and ry is the radius perpendicular to the current direction. The program (ellip1.nll) shows two ways to draw two ellipses of the same kind oriented perpendicular to each other. With the E1 command string a turn of $\pi/2$ is made to draw the second ellipse. With the E2 command string the rx and ry values are swapped for the second ellipse which has the same effect.

Program (ellip1.nll)

```
rx = 2;
ry = 1;
E1 : P(2,2) E(rx,ry) T(pi/2) E(rx,ry);
E2 : P(2,2) E(rx,ry) E(ry,rx);
```

Command line
```
nell ellip1.nll E1 3 | nellsvg 4 4 in 0.02 1 > ellip1.svg
nell ellip1.nll E2 3 | nellsvg 4 4 in 0.02 1 > ellip1.svg
```

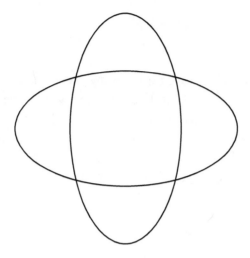

You can also create Moire patterns with sets of equally spaced concentric ellipses. The patterns are similar to those created with circles but there are differences. The program (`ellip2.nll`) will draw two sets of 40 concentric ellipses spaced a small horizontal distance apart.

Program (`ellip2.nll`)

```
n = 40;
rx = 0.05;
ry = 0.025;
drx = rx;
dry = ry;
T1 : E(rx,ry) A(rx,rx+drx) A(ry,ry+dry);
START : P(2.05,2.05) S(T1,n) A(rx,drx) A(ry,dry) M(4*drx) S(T1,n)
```

Command line
```
nell ellip2.nll START 3 | nellsvg 4.3 2.1 in 0.02 1 > ellip2.svg
```

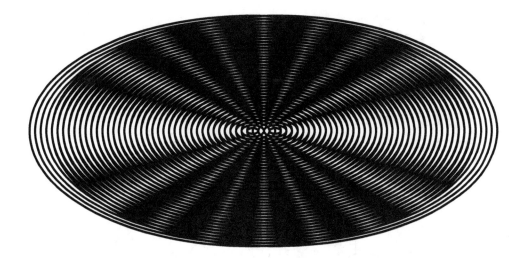

A circle can be defined as all points whose distance from a point, called the center of the circle, is a constant value. Likewise an ellipse can be defined as all points whose distances from two points, called the foci of the ellipse, have a constant sum. The two foci are located on the long axis of the ellipse. If rx>ry then the foci are located a distance c=sqrt(rx^2-ry^2) from the center of the ellipse. The following program will draw n ellipses rotated about a common focus with a circle surrounding them all (ellip3.nll):

Program (ellip3.nll)

```
n = 48;
a = 2*pi/n;
rx = 1.5;
ry = 3/4;
c = sqrt(rx^2-ry^2);
E1 : [M(c) E(rx,ry)] T(a);
START : P(rx+c+0.04,rx+c+0.04) S(E1,n) C(rx+c);
```

Command line

```
nell ellip3.nll START 3 | nellsvg 5.7 5.7 in 0.02 1 > ellip3.svg
```

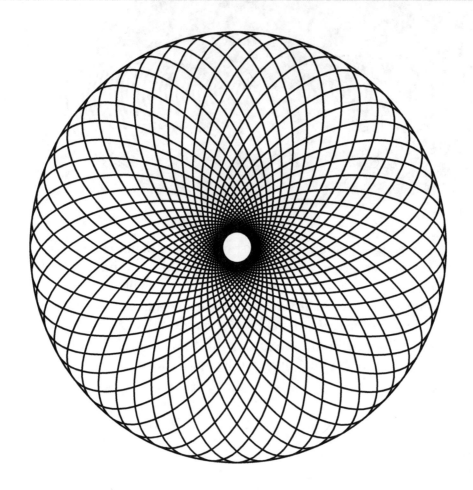

ARCS

You can create both circular and elliptic arcs with the R(rx,ry,a,da) command. For a circular arc set rx=ry. The arc is centered at the current position and its starting point is at angle a from the current direction. Positive angles are to the left of the current direction (counterclockwise) and negative angles are to the right (clockwise). The angle swept out by the arc from the starting to the ending point is da. The command R(1,1,-pi/2,pi) will draw a half circle of radius 1. The program (arc1.nll) will draw a half circle on each side of a square.

Program (arc1.nll)

```
T1 : L(1) T(pi/2);
T2 : [M(0.5) T(-pi/2) R(0.5,0.5,-pi/2,pi)] M(1) T(pi/2);
START : P(0.5,0.5) <S(T1,3) Z()> S(T2,4);
```

Command line
```
nell arc1.nll START 10 | nellsvg 2 2 in 0.02 1 > arc1.svg
```

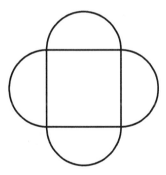

This can be generalized to drawing a half circle on each side of an n-sided polygon. Program (`arc2.nll`) shows how to do it but without drawing the sides of the polygon.

Program (`arc2.nll`)

```
n = 5;
a = 2*pi/n;
T1 : L(1) T(pi/2);
T2 : [M(0.5) T(-pi/2) R(0.5,0.5,-pi/2,pi)] M(1) T(a);
START : P(0.75,0.5) S(T2,n);
```

Command line
```
nell arc2.nll START 3 | nellsvg 2.5 2.3 in 0.02 1 > arc2.svg
```

The program (`arc3.nll`) is basically the same as (`arc2.nll`) but it draws a half ellipse instead of a half circle. The radius of the ellipse extending away from the center is three times the radius along the edges.

Program (`arc3.nll`)

```
n = 6;
```

```
a = 2*pi/n;
T1 : L(1) T(pi/2);
T2 : [M(0.5) T(-pi/2) R(1.5,0.5,-pi/2,pi)] M(1) T(a);
START : P(1.6,1.5) S(T2,n);
```

Command line

```
nell arc3.nll START 3 | nellsvg 4.2 4.8 in 0.02 1 > arc3.svg
```

The program (`arc4.nll`) draws elliptic arcs at evenly spaced angles around a common center.

Program (`arc4.nll`)

```
n = 24;
a = 2*pi/n;
T1 : R(1.5,0.5,-0.38,pi/2) T(a);
START : P(1.55,1.55) S(T1,n) C(0.73);
```

Command line
```
nell arc4.nll START 3 | nellsvg 3.1 3.1 in 0.02 1 > arc4.svg
```

The program (`arc5.nll`) draws a crescent using circular arcs.

Program (`arc5.nll`)

```
a = 5*pi/8;
START : P(0.6,1.15) R(1,1,-pi/2,pi) M(0.4) R(1.1,1.1,-a,2*a);
```

Command line
```
nell arc5.nll START 3 | nellsvg 2.25 2.3 in 0.02 1 > arc5.svg
```

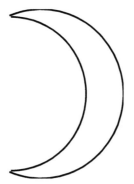

BEZIER CURVES

You can draw quadratic Bezier curves with the command Q(l,lc,ac). The variable l is the straight line distance, in the current direction, to the point the curve will connect to. The variable lc is the distance to the control point which is at an angle ac with respect to the current direction. For positive ac this is counterclockwise from the current direction and for negative ac it is clockwise. If you draw lines from the curve start and end points to the control point then the curve will start and end tangent to those lines.

The program (bezier1.nll) draws a quadratic Bezier curve between two points and it draws lines from the start and end of the curve to the control point so you can see how the curve is tangent to the lines. The command Q(1,1.5,ac) indicates that the straight line distance between the start and end points is 1. The distance of the control point from the start point is 1.5 and the direction of the control point is ac which is set to pi/6.

Program (bezier1.nll)

```
l = 1;
lc = 1.5;
ac = pi/6;
lp = sqrt(l^2+lc^2-2*l*lc*cos(ac));
ap = pi-asin(lc*sin(ac)/lp);
START : P(0.1,0.1) T(pi/6) [T(ac) L(lc) T(-ac-ap) L(lp)] Q(1,1.5,ac);
```

Command line
nell bezier1.nll START 3 | nellsvg 1.25 1.5 in 0.015 1 > bezier1.svg

One of the nice things you can do with a Bezier curve is draw an exact parabola. Program (`bezier2.nll`) draws four parabolas between the same two points separated by distance l=2. The parabolas are of the form $y = ax^2$ for a=2, 1, 1/2, 1/4.

Program (`bezier2.nll`)

```
a = 2;
l = 2;
P1 : [Q(l,(1/2)*sqrt(a^2*l^2+1),atan(-a*l))] A(a,a/2);
START : P(0,2) S(P1,4);
```

Command line

```
nell bezier2.nll START 3 | nellsvg 2 2 in 0.015 1 > bezier2.svg
```

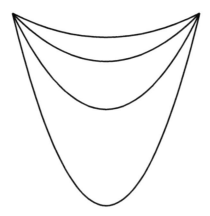

Using parabolas you can create a very close approximation to a sine function. Program (`bezier3.nll`) draws an approximation of three periods of a sine function. Each half period is actually a parabola. The same control point distance is used for each parabola but the control point angles alternate in sign.

Program (bezier3.nll)

```
a = 4;
l = 1;
lc = (1/2)*sqrt(a^2*l^2+1);
ac = atan(-a*l);
P1 : Q(l,lc,-ac) Q(l,lc,ac);
START : P(0,1) S(P1,3);
```

Command line
```
nell bezier3.nll START 3 | nellsvg 6 2 in 0.02 1 > bezier3.svg
```

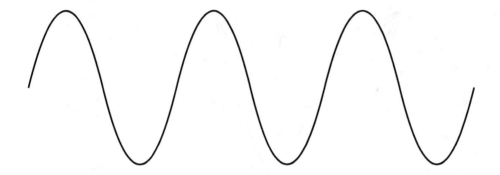

The program (`bezier4.nll`) draws a heart shaped object. You can experiment with different shapes by changing the values of `lc` and `ac`.

Program (`bezier4.nll`)

```
lc = 3;
ac = pi/5;
START : M(1) T(pi/2) [Q(1,lc,ac)] Q(1,lc,-ac);
```

Command line
```
nell bezier4.nll START 3 | nellsvg 2 2 in 0.02 1 > bezier4.svg
```

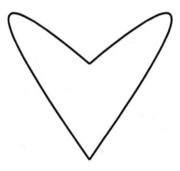

The program (`bezier5.nll`) draws a flower like object.

Program (`bezier5.nll`)

```
T1 : [Q(1,2,pi/10) M(0.25) C(0.1)] [Q(1,2,-pi/10)];
T2 : S(T1,1) T(pi/5);
START : P(1.4,1.4) S(T2,10);
```

Command line
```
nell bezier5.nll START 3 | nellsvg 2.8 2.8 in 0.02 1 > bezier5.svg
```

The program (`clover.nll`) draws a four leaf clover.

Program (`clover.nll`)

```
l = 1;
lc = 1.75;
ac = 0.22*pi;
as = -3*pi/4+ac/2; stem angle
das = 0.02; controls stem width
LEAF : [Q(l,lc,ac)] [Q(l,lc,-ac)];
T1 : S(LEAF,1) T(pi/2);
STEM : [T(as-das) Q(2,1.5,-pi/8)] T(as+das) Q(2,1.5,-pi/8);
START : P(1.25,1.75) T(pi/3) S(T1,4) S(STEM,1);
```

Command line
```
nell clover.nll START 3 | nellsvg 2.6 3 in 0.02 1 > clover.svg
```

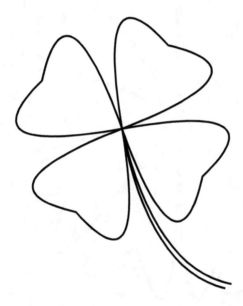

You can draw cubic Bezier curves with the command B(1,lc1,ac1,lc2,ac2).
The command is very similar to the quadratic Bezier command but with

one extra control point whose distance and direction are with respect to the end point of the curve. The extra control point allows more complicated curves to be drawn. As in the quadratic curve, the variable l is the straight line distance, in the current direction, to the point the curve will connect to. lc1 and ac1 are the distance and direction of the first control point with respect to the start of the curve while lc2 and ac2 are the distance and direction of the second control point with respect to the end of the curve. If you draw lines from the start of the curve to the first control point and from the end of the curve to the second control point then the curve will be tangent to those lines at the start and end.

The program (bezier6.nll) draws a cubic Bezier curve between two points and it draws lines from the start and end of the curve to the control points so you can see how the curve is tangent to the lines. The straight line distance between the start and end points is 1. The distance to both control points is 2 but note that for the second control point the distance is negative which has the effect of flipping the direction 180 degrees or π radians.

Program (bezier6.nll)

```
l = 1;
lc1 = 2;
ac1 = pi/6;
lc2 = -2;
ac2 = pi/6;
START : P(0.5,1) [T(ac1) L(lc1)] B(l,lc1,ac1,lc2,ac2) [T(ac2) L(lc2)];
```

Command line
```
nell bezier6.nll START 3 | nellsvg 2 2 in 0.02 1 > bezier6.svg
```

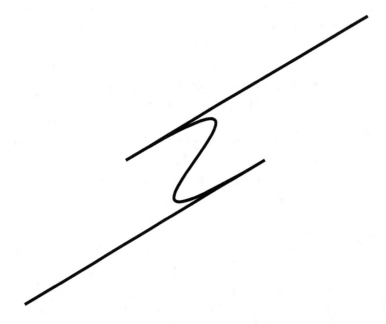

The program (bezier7.nll) is basically the same as (bezier6.nll) but with the sign on ac2 negative. This has a dramatic effect on the shape of the curve.

Program (bezier7.nll)

```
l = 1;
lc1 = 2;
ac1 = pi/6;
lc2 = -2;
ac2 = -pi/6;
START : P(0.5,1) [T(ac1) L(lc1)] B(l,lc1,ac1,lc2,ac2) [T(ac2) L(lc2)];
```

Command line
```
nell bezier7.nll START 3 | nellsvg 2 2 in 0.02 1 > bezier7.svg
```

The program (`bezier8.nll`) draws a Bezier curve between the vertices of an n-sided polygon.

Program (`bezier8.nll`)

```
n = 7;
a = 2*pi/n;
l = 1;
lc1 = 2;
ac1 = pi/6;
lc2 = -2;
ac2 = -pi/6;
T1 : B(l,lc1,ac1,lc2,ac2) T(a);
START : P(0.75,0) S(T1,n);
```

Command line
```
nell bezier8.nll START 3 | nellsvg 2.5 2.25 in 0.02 1 > bezier8.svg
```

The program (`bezier9.nll`) is the same as (`bezier8.nll`) but with different parameter values.

Program (`bezier9.nll`)

```
n = 4;
a = 2*pi/n;
l = 2;
lc1 = 4;
ac1 = pi/6;
lc2 = -4;
ac2 = -pi/6;
T1 : B(l,lc1,ac1,lc2,ac2) T(a);
START : S(T1,n);
```

Command line

```
nell bezier9.nll START 3 | nellsvg 2 2 in 0.02 1 > bezier9.svg
```

GALLERY

This section of the book is a collection of Nell program examples that serve as a handy reference and quick start for creating a drawing you need to make now. To really understand a language you should read a lot of code examples to fully grasp its capabilities. All the program files can be found on the book's website.

Program (`koch.nll`) Note that line labeled `T1` is broken here but is one line in the actual file.

```
; Creates a Koch curve whose generation is specified by
; the command line recursion level.
a = pi/3;
l = 0.025;
T1 : L(l) S(T1,1) L(l) T(a) L(l) S(T1,1) L(l) T(-2*a) L(l) S(T1,1)
     L(l) T(a) L(l) S(T1,1) L(l);
```

Command line
```
nell koch.nll T1 3 | nellsvg 6 2 in 0.02 1 > koch.svg
```

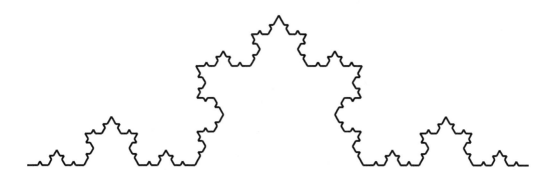

Program (`hilbert.nll`)

```
; Creates a Hilbert curve whose generation is specified by
; the command line recursion level.
b = pi/2;
s = 0.2;
A : T(b) S(B,1) L(s) T(-b) S(A,1) L(s) S(A,1) T(-b) L(s) S(B,1) T(b);
B : T(-b) S(A,1) L(s) T(b) S(B,1) L(s) S(B,1) T(b) L(s) S(A,1) T(-b);
START : <S(A,1)>;
```

Command line
```
nell hilbert.nll START 5 | nellsvg 6.2 6.2 in 0.02 1 > hilbert.svg
```

Program (`peano.nll`) Note that line labeled `T1` is broken here but is one line in the actual file.

```
; Creates a Peano curve.
a = pi/4;
l = .0625;
T1 : S(T1,1) L(l) S(TP,1) S(T1,1) L(l) S(TN,1) S(T1,1) L(l) S(TN,1)
     S(T1,1) L(l) S(TN,1) S(T1,1) L(l) S(TP,1) S(T1,1) L(l) S(TP,1)
     S(T1,1) L(l) S(TP,1) S(T1,1) L(l) S(TN,1) S(T1,1);
TP : T(a) L(4*l) T(a);
TN : T(-a) L(4*l) T(-a);
START : P(0,12.0) <S(T1,1) L(l)>;
```

Command line
```
nell peano.nll START 4 | nellsvg 25 24 cm 0.1 1 > peano.svg
```

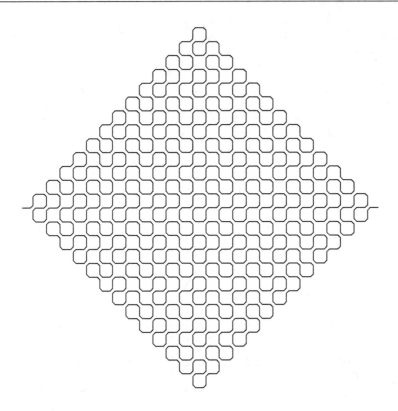

Program (`sierpinski.nll`) Note that line labeled **T1** is broken here but is one line in the actual file.

```
; A Sierpinski triangle.
a = 2*pi/3;
l = 4;
T1 : A(1,1/2) S(T1,1) A(1,2*1) L(1) T(a) A(1,1/2) S(T1,1) A(1,2*1)
     L(1) T(a) A(1,1/2) S(T1,1) A(1,2*1) L(1) T(a);
PIC : P(-1/2+2,-1/2+2) S(T1,1);
```

Command line
```
nell sierpinski.nll PIC 6 | nellsvg 4 3.5 in 0.005 1 > sierpinski.svg
```

Program (cairo.nll)

```
; Produces a tiling with irregular pentagons called a Cairo tiling.
n = 6;
l = 0.25;
a = pi/3;
b = pi/2;
d = sqrt(3)-1;
T1 : L(l*d) T(a) L(l) T(b) L(l) T(a) L(l) T(b) L(l) T(a);
T2 : L(l*d) T(-a) L(l) T(-b) L(l) T(-a) L(l) T(-b) L(l) T(-a);
T3 : L(l) T(b) L(l) T(a) L(l*d) T(a) L(l) T(b) L(l) T(a);
T4 : S(T1,1) S(T2,1) T(2*a) S(T3,1) T(-2*a) M(l*d) T(-a) S(T3,1) T(a);
T5 : S(T4,1) T(a) M(2*l) T(-a) S(T4,1);
```

```
T6 : [S(T5,1)] M(2*sqrt(3)*l);
T7 : [S(T6,n)] T(b) M(2*sqrt(3)*l) T(-b);
PIC : P(0.35,0.35) S(T7,n);
```

Command line
```
nell cairo.nll PIC 10 | nellsvg 5.75 5.5 in 0.02 1 > cairo.svg
```

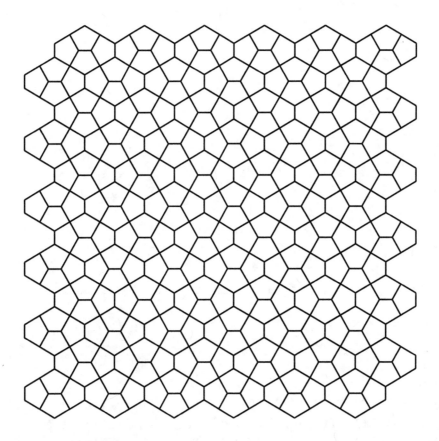

Program (`tatami.nll`) Note that line labeled T2 is broken here but is one line in the actual file.

```
; Creates a tatami mat.
a = -pi/2;
l = 5;
n = 6;
i = 0;
T1 : L(2*l) T(a) L(l) T(a) L(2*l) T(a) L(l) T(a) M(2*l);
T2 : S(T1,i) M(l) T(a) S(T1,i) M(l) T(a) S(T1,i) M(l) T(a) S(T1,i)
     M(l) T(a);
T3 : T(-pi/4) M(-l*sqrt(2)) T(pi/4) A(i,i+1) S(T2,l);
PIC : P(35,35) T(-pi/4) M(-l/sqrt(2)) T(pi/4) S(T3,n);
```

Command line

```
nell tatami.nll PIC 5 | nellsvg 70 70 mm 0.2 1 > tatami.svg
```

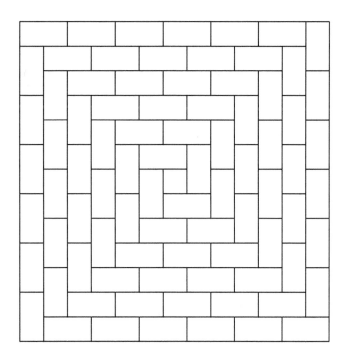

Program (`trellis1.nll`) Note that line labeled T1 is broken here but is one line in the actual file.

```
; Creates a trellis pattern.
l = 0;
lc1 = 0.7;
ac1 = 0.9;
lc2 = -0.7;
ac2 = -0.9;
y = 0.85;
h = sqrt(11)/10;
T1 : M(0.5) [T(pi/2) M(h) T(-pi/2) B(l,lc1,ac1,lc2,ac2)]
     [T(-pi/2) M(h) T(pi/2) B(l,lc1,-ac1,lc2,-ac2)] M(0.5);
T2 : S(T1,1) C(0.4) C(0.6) E(0.4,0.1) E(0.1,0.4);
T3 : P(-0.75,y) S(T2,8) S(T1,1) A(y,y+1.5);
START : S(T3,6);
```

Command line
```
nell trellis1.nll START 3 | nellsvg 7.5 9.25 in 0.02 1 > trellis1.svg
```

Program (spiral.nll)

```
d = 0.025;
a = pi/8;
```

```
T1 : L(d) T(a);
ARM : S(T1,8) A(d,d+0.025);
START : P(2.55,2.55) <S(ARM,40)>;
```

Command line
```
nell spiral.nll START 3 | nellsvg 5.1 5.1 in 0.02 1 > spiral.svg
```

Program (ladybug.nll) Note that lines labeled ANTENNA, HEAD, FSPOTS, BSPOTS, and START are broken here but are one line each in the actual file.

```
; Draws a lady bug.
```

```
MOUTH : M(-0.4) R(0.3,0.1,0,-pi);
EYE : T(pi/2) M(0.2) C(0.05);
ANTENNA : T(pi/2) M(0.5) [Q(0.5,0.5,-pi/12) C(0.03)] T(-pi/2) M(0.1)
          T(pi/2) [Q(0.5,0.5,-pi/12) C(0.03)];
HEAD : R(0.7,0.5,0,pi) R(0.7,0.3,0,-pi) [S(MOUTH,1) S(EYE,1)]
       S(ANTENNA,1);
BODY : R(1.2,1,0,pi) R(1.2,0.35,0,-pi) R(1.2,0.7,0,pi);
FLEG : M(-1.2) T(-2*pi/3) Q(1,1,pi/3); front leg
MLEG : T(-pi/2) M(0.35) T(-pi/8) Q(0.6,0.62,pi/8); middle leg
BLEG : M(1.2) T(-pi/3) Q(1,1,-pi/3); back leg
FSPOTS : P(1.95,2.2) C(0.15) P(2.5,1.9) C(0.15) P(3.6,2.0) C(0.15)
         P(3.0,2.5) C(0.15); foreground spots
BSPOTS : P(1.8,2.4) T(2*pi/5) R(0.08,0.08,pi,7*pi/8) P(2.5,2.85)
         C(0.08) P(3.6,2.7) C(0.08) P(3.0,2.83)
         C(0.1); background spots
START : P(1,2) [S(HEAD,1)] M(1.9) S(BODY,1) [S(FSPOTS,1)]
        [S(BSPOTS,1)] [S(FLEG,1)] [S(MLEG,1)] [S(BLEG,1)];
```

Command line

```
nell ladybug.nll START 3 | nellsvg 6 5 in 0.02 1 > ladybug.svg
```

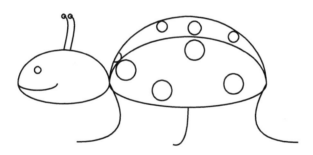

Program (tess03.nll)

```
; Creates a triangle tesselation.
a = 2*pi/3;
d = sqrt(2*(1-cos(a)));
T1 : L(d) T(5*a/4) L(1) T(a/2) L(1) T(a) L(1) T(a/2) L(1) T(3*a/4);
T2 : L(d) T(a) L(d);
PIC : P(1,0.65) S(T1,3) T(-a/4) M(1) T(a/4) S(T2,3);
```

Command line
```
nell tess03.nll PIC 5 | nellsvg 3.7 3.25 cm 0.01 1 > tess03.svg
```

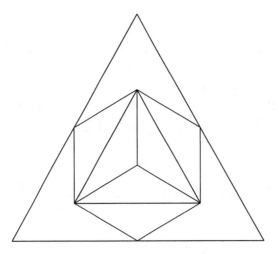

Program (tess05.nll) Note that line labeled PIC is broken here but is one line in the actual file.

```
; Creates a pentagon tesselation.
a = 2*pi/5;
d1 = sqrt(2*(1-cos(a)));
d2 = sqrt(2*(1-cos(2*a)));
T1 : L(d1) T(7*a/4) L(1) T(3*a/2) L(1) T(a) L(1) T(3*a/2) L(1) T(a/4);
```

```
T2 : L(d2) T(9*a/4) L(1) T(a/2) L(1) T(2*a) L(1) T(a/2) L(1) T(3*a/4);
T3 : L(d1) T(a) L(d1);
PIC : P(1.4,1.3) S(T1,5) T(-3*a/4) M(1) T(5*a/4) S(T2,5) T(-a/4) M(1)
      T(a/4) S(T3,5);
```

Command line

```
nell tess05.nll PIC 5 | nellsvg 4 3.9 cm 0.01 1 > tess05.svg
```

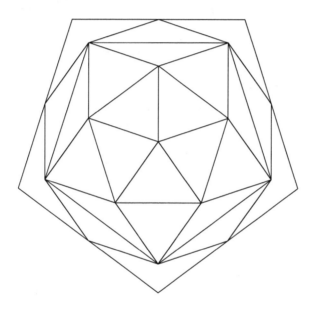

Program (`tess06.nll`) Note that line labeled `PIC` is broken here but is one line in the actual file.

```
; Creates a hexagon tesselation.
a = pi/3;
d1 = sqrt(2*(1-cos(a)));
d2 = sqrt(2*(1-cos(2*a)));
```

```
d3 = 2/sqrt(3);
T1 : L(d1) T(2*a) L(1) T(2*a) L(1) T(a) L(1) T(2*a) L(1);
T2 : L(d2) T(5*a/2) L(1) T(a) L(1) T(2*a) L(1) T(a) L(1) T(a/2);
T3 : L(d3) T(a) L(d3);
PIC : P(1.6,1.5) S(T1,6) T(-a) M(1) T(3*a/2) S(T2,6) T(-a/2) M(1)
      T(a/2) S(T3,6);
```

Command line

```
nell tess06.nll PIC 5 | nellsvg 4.2 4.7 cm 0.01 1 > tess06.svg
```

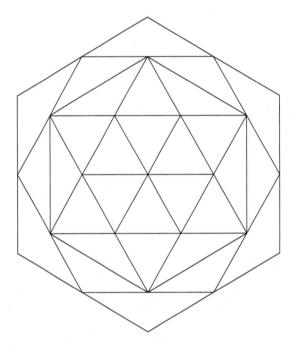

Program (tess08.nll) Note that line labeled PIC is broken here but is one line in the actual file.

```
; Creates an octagon tesselation.
```

```
a = pi/4;
d1 = sqrt(2*(1-cos(a)));
d2 = sqrt(2*(1-cos(2*a)));
d3 = sqrt(2*(1-cos(3*a)));
T1 : L(d1) T(5*a/2) L(1) T(3*a) L(1) T(a) L(1) T(3*a) L(1) T(-a/2);
T2 : L(d2) T(3*a) L(1) T(2*a) L(1) T(2*a) L(1) T(2*a) L(1);
T3 : L(d3) T(7*a/2) L(1) T(a) L(1) T(3*a) L(1) T(a) L(1) T(a/2);
PIC : P(2.3,1.8) S(T1,8) T(-3*a/2) M(1) T(2*a) S(T2,8) T(-a) M(1)
      T(3*a/2) S(T3,8);
```

Command line
```
nell tess08.nll PIC 5 | nellsvg 5.4 5.4 cm 0.01 1 > tess08.svg
```

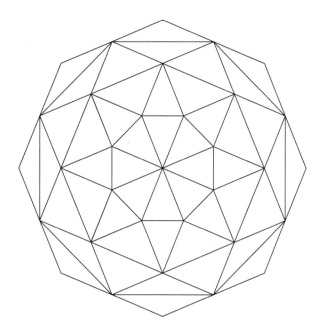

Program (`tess10.nll`) Note that line labeled `PIC` is broken here but is one line in the actual file.

```
; Creates a decagon tesselation.
a = pi/5;
d1 = sqrt(2*(1-cos(a)));
d2 = sqrt(2*(1-cos(2*a)));
d3 = sqrt(2*(1-cos(3*a)));
d4 = sqrt(2*(1-cos(4*a)));
T1 : L(d1) T(3*a) L(1) T(4*a) L(1) T(a) L(1) T(4*a) L(1) T(-a);
T2 : L(d2) T(7*a/2) L(1) T(3*a) L(1) T(2*a) L(1) T(3*a) L(1) T(-a/2);
T3 : L(d3) T(4*a) L(1) T(2*a) L(1) T(3*a) L(1) T(2*a) L(1);
T4 : L(d4) T(9*a/2) L(1) T(a) L(1) T(4*a) L(1) T(a) L(1) T(a/2);
PIC : P(3,2.3) S(T1,10) T(-2*a) M(1) T(5*a/2) S(T2,10) T(-3*a/2) M(1)
      T(2*a) S(T3,10) T(-a) M(1) T(3*a/2) S(T4,10);
```

Command line

```
nell tess10.nll PIC 5 | nellsvg 6.6 6.5 cm 0.01 1 > tess10.svg
```

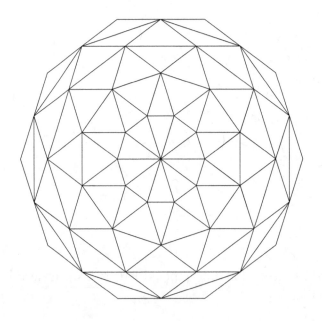

Program (`tess16.nll`) Note that line labeled `PIC` is broken here but is one line in the actual file.

```
; Creates a 16-gon tesselation.
a = pi/8;
d1 = sqrt(2*(1-cos(a)));
d2 = sqrt(2*(1-cos(2*a)));
d3 = sqrt(2*(1-cos(3*a)));
d4 = sqrt(2*(1-cos(4*a)));
d5 = sqrt(2*(1-cos(5*a)));
d6 = sqrt(2*(1-cos(6*a)));
d7 = sqrt(2*(1-cos(7*a)));
T1 : L(d1) T(9*a/2) L(1) T(7*a) L(1) T(a) L(1) T(7*a) L(1) T(-5*a/2);
T2 : L(d2) T(5*a) L(1) T(6*a) L(1) T(2*a) L(1) T(6*a) L(1) T(-2*a);
T3 : L(d3) T(11*a/2) L(1) T(5*a) L(1) T(3*a) L(1) T(5*a) L(1) T(-3*a/2);
T4 : L(d4) T(6*a) L(1) T(4*a) L(1) T(4*a) L(1) T(4*a) L(1) T(-a);
T5 : L(d5) T(13*a/2) L(1) T(3*a) L(1) T(5*a) L(1) T(3*a) L(1) T(-a/2);
T6 : L(d6) T(7*a) L(1) T(2*a) L(1) T(6*a) L(1) T(2*a) L(1) T(0);
T7 : L(d7) T(15*a/2) L(1) T(a) L(1) T(7*a) L(1) T(a) L(1) T(a/2);
PIC : P(5.05,4.25) S(T1,16) T(-7*a/2) M(1) T(4*a) S(T2,16) T(-3*a)
        M(1) T(7*a/2) S(T3,16) T(-5*a/2) M(1) T(3*a) S(T4,16) T(-2*a)
        M(1) T(5*a/2) S(T5,16) T(-3*a/2) M(1) T(2*a) S(T6,16) T(-a)
        M(1) T(3*a/2) S(T7,16);
```

Command line
```
nell tess16.nll PIC 5 | nellsvg 10.5 10.5 cm 0.01 1 > tess16.svg
```

Program (`tile005.nll`) Note that line labeled **T2** is broken here but is one line in the actual file.

```
; Creates a tiling using octagons
a = pi/4;
d = 1;
d1 = 1 + sqrt(2);
d2 = 2 + sqrt(2);
T1 : L(1) T(a);
T2 : <S(T1,7) Z()> T(a) M(d*d1) T(-a) <S(T1,7) Z()> T(-a) M(d*d1)
```

```
      T(a);
T3 : [S(T2,4)] T(2*a) M(d*d2) T(-2*a);
START : M(1) S(T3,4);
```

Command line
```
nell tile005.nll START 10 | nellsvg 15 15 cm 0.05 1 > tile005.svg
```

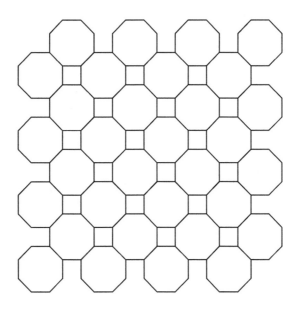

Program (tile006.nll)

```
; Creates a square in center alternating with squares and pentagons.
l = 10;
a = 2*pi/4;
b = 2*pi/5;
T1 : L(l) T(b) L(l) T(b) S(T2,1) L(l) T(b) S(T2,1) L(l) T(b) L(l) T(b);
T2 : L(l) T(-a) L(l) T(-a) S(T1,1) L(l) T(-a) L(l) T(-a);
```

```
PIC : P(100,100) T(a/2) M(-1/sqrt(2)) T(-a/2) S(T2,1) M(1) T(a)
      S(T2,1) M(1) T(a) S(T2,1) M(1) T(a) S(T2,1) M(1) T(a)
      P(100,100) C(8.7*1-2.5) C(8.7*1);
```

Command line

```
nell tile006.nll PIC 7 | nellsvg 200 200 mm 0.5 1 > tile006.svg
```

Program (tile007.nll) Note that lines labeled T2, and PIC are broken here but are one line each in the actual file.

```
; Creates pentagon in center alternating with rectangles and pentagons.
1 = 5;
```

```
a = 2*pi/5;
b = 2*pi/5;
T1 : L(1) T(b) L(1) T(b) S(T2,1) L(1) T(b) S(T2,1) L(1) T(b) L(1) T(b);
T2 : L(1) T(-pi/2) L(2*1) T(-pi/2) S(T1,1) L(1) T(-pi/2) L(2*1)
     T(-pi/2);
PIC : P(66,66) T(3*pi/10) M(-1/(2*cos(3*pi/10))) T(-3*pi/10) S(T2,1)
      M(1) T(a) S(T2,1) M(1) T(a) S(T2,1) M(1) T(a) S(T2,1) M(1) T(a)
      S(T2,1) M(1) T(a) P(66,66) C(13*1-2.5) C(13*1);
```

Command line
```
nell tile007.nll PIC 7 | nellsvg 132 132 mm 0.5 1 > tile007.svg
```

Program (`tile008.nll`) Note that lines labeled `T1`, `T2`, and `PIC` are broken here but are one line each in the actual file.

```
; Creates hexagon in center alternating with rectangles and hexagons.
l = 5;
a = pi/3;
T1 : L(l) T(a) S(T2,1) L(l) T(a) S(T2,1) L(l) T(a) S(T2,1) L(l) T(a)
     S(T2,1) L(l) T(a) L(l) T(a);
T2 : L(l) T(-pi/2) L(2*l) T(-pi/2) S(T1,1) L(l) T(-pi/2) L(2*l)
     T(-pi/2);
PIC : P(55,62) T(a) M(-l) T(-a) S(T2,1) M(l) T(a) S(T2,1) M(l) T(a)
      S(T2,1) M(l) T(a) S(T2,1) M(l) T(a) S(T2,1) M(l) T(a) S(T2,1)
      M(l) T(a);
```

Command line

```
nell tile008.nll PIC 6 | nellsvg 110 124 mm 0.5 1 > tile008.svg
```

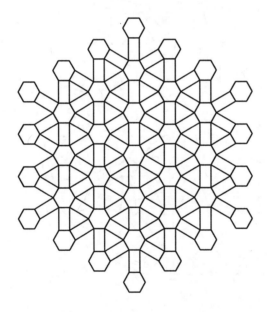

Program (tile009.nll)

```
; Creates a pattern with equilateral triangles.
l1 = 10;
l2 = 5;
a = 2*pi/3;
n = 2;
T1 : L(l1) T(a) L(l1) T(a) L(l1) T(a) M(l1+l2) S(T1,1);
T2 : [S(T1,1)] T(pi/3) M(l1+l2) T(-pi/3);
T3 : [S(T2,n)] T(pi/6);
PIC : P(38,38) S(T3,12) C(25) C(37); C(50);
```

Command line

```
nell tile009.nll PIC 4 | nellsvg 76 76 mm 0.5 1 > tile009.svg
```

Program (`tile011.nll`) Note that line labeled `T1` is broken here but is one line in the actual file.

```
; Creates a pattern with hexagons.
l1 = 10;
l2 = 10;
a = pi/3;
n = 2;
T1 : L(l1) T(a) L(l1) T(a) L(l1) T(a) L(l1) T(a) L(l1) T(a) L(l1)
     T(3*a/2) M(l1*sqrt(3)+l2) T(-a/2) S(T1,1);
T2 : [S(T1,1)] T(pi/2) M(l1*sqrt(3)+l2) T(-pi/2);
T3: [S(T2,n)] T(pi/6);
PIC: P(72,72) S(T3,12) C(70.0);
```

Command line
```
nell tile011.nll PIC 4 | nellsvg 144 144 mm 0.5 1 > tile011.svg
```

Program (`tile012.nll`) Note that line labeled H2 is broken here but is one line in the actual file.

```
; Creates a tiling using dodecagons.
; d = tile spacing
; d < 1 tiles overlap
; d = 1 exact tiling
; d > 1 tiles space apart
; d = 0.5 produces an interesting tiling
a = pi/6;
d = sqrt(3)-1;
d0 = 2+sqrt(3);
d1 = sqrt(3)*d0;
n = 6;
ah = pi/3;
dh = 0.5;
h1 = sqrt(2*(1-cos(ah)))/2;
h2 = sqrt(2*(1-cos(2*ah)))/2;
H1 : L(h1) T(2*ah) L(dh) T(2*ah) L(dh) T(ah) L(dh) T(2*ah) L(dh);
H2 : L(h2) T(5*ah/2) L(dh) T(ah) L(dh) T(2*ah) L(dh) T(ah) L(dh)
     T(ah/2);
HP : T(ah/2) S(H1,6) T(-ah) M(dh) T(3*ah/2) S(H2,6);
T0 : L(1) T(a);
T1 : S(T0,12) [T(pi/3) M(1) T(pi/6) M(dh) T(-pi/2) S(HP,1)];
T2 : S(T1,1) T(2*a) M(d*d0) T(-2*a) S(T1,1);
T3 : [S(T2,1)] M(d*d0);
T4 : [S(T3,n)] T(pi/2) M(d*d1) T(-pi/2);
PIC : S(T4,n/2);
```

Command line
```
nell tile012.nll PIC 10 | nellsvg 16 16 cm 0.02 1 > tile012.svg
```

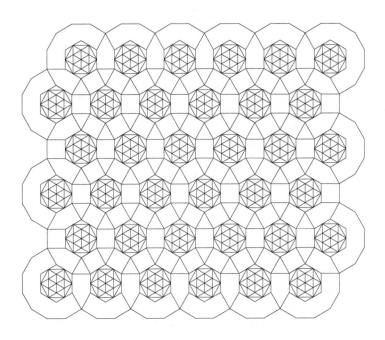

Program (triadcirc.nll)

```
; Creates the circle of major triads.
a = pi/6;
l = 1;
T0 : C(l/4) M(l/2);
T1 : [<L(3*l/4)> M(l/4) S(T0,3)] T(a);
PIC : P(2.3,2.3) C(3*l/4) C(5*l/4) C(7*l/4) C(9*l/4) S(T1,12);
```

Command line
```
nell triadcirc.nll PIC 6 | nellsvg 4.6 4.6 in 0.01 1 > triadcirc.svg
```

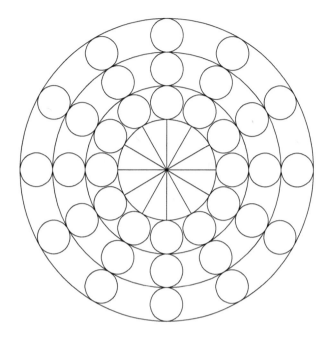

Program (`horns.nll`) Note that lines labeled L3, R3 and PIC are broken here but are one line each in the actual file.

```
; horns.pen creates a pair of spiral horns composed of squares and
; triangles. The length of the horns depends on the value of n.
n = 30; n determines length of horns.
A = 5;
B = 12;
C = 13;
a = A;
b = B;
c = C;
s = b/c;
t1 = pi-angle(a,b,c);
t2 = pi-angle(b,c,a);
```

```
t3 = pi-angle(c,a,b);
t4 = -pi/2;
t5 = -2*pi/3;
L1 : L(c) T(t4) L(c) T(t4) L(c) T(t4) L(c) T(t4); left square
L2 : L(c) T(t3) L(a) T(t1) L(b) T(t2);              left triangle
L3 : S(L1,1) S(L2,1) A(a,s*a) A(b,s*b) A(c,s*c) T(3*pi/2-t2) M(c)
     T(-pi/2);
R1 : L(c) T(t4) L(c) T(t4) L(c) T(t4) L(c) T(t4); right square
R2 : L(c) T(t2) L(b) T(t1) L(a) T(t3);              right triangle
R3 : S(R1,1) S(R2,1) A(a,s*a) A(b,s*b) A(c,s*c) T(pi-t3) M((a+b)/s)
     T(-pi/2);
T1 : L(2*c) T(t5) L(2*c) T(t5) L(2*c) T(t5);
PIC : P(70,36) M(-c) [S(L3,n)] A(a,A) A(b,B) A(c,C) M(c) [S(R3,n)]
      A(a,A) A(b,B) A(c,C) P(70-c,36-c) S(T1,1);
```

Command line

```
nell horns.nll PIC 10 | nellsvg 140 70 mm 0.2 1 > horns.svg
```

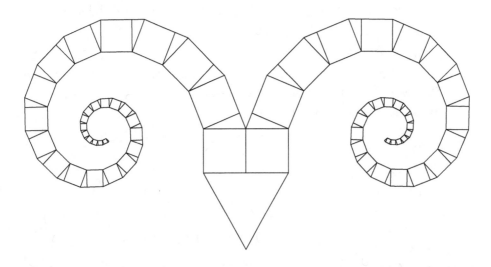

Program (network.nll)

```
; Creates a network of resistors.
a = pi/3;
b = 2*a;
l1 = 0.25;
l2 = l1/2;
V : T(-b) L(l1) T(b) L(l1);
R : L(l1) T(a) L(l2) S(V,2) T(-b) L(l1) T(b) L(l2) T(-a) L(l1);
SRC :  L(l1+l2) M(l1) C(l1) M(l1) L(l1+l2);
T : S(R,1) [T(-pi/2) S(R,1)];
START : P(l1,1.375) [S(T,3)] P(l1,.125) [S(R,3)] T(pi/2) S(SRC,1);
```

Command line

```
nell network.nll START 3 | nellsvg 4.125 1.5 in 0.02 1 > network.svg
```

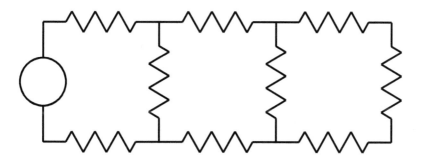

Program (prism.nll) Note that line labeled CALC is broken here but is one line in the actual file.

```
; This shows the dispersion of light through an isosceles prism.
n0 = 1; air index of refraction
n1 = 1.6; prism index of refraction
phi = pi/3; apex angle
psi = (pi-phi)/2; base interior angle
```

```
a = (pi+phi)/2; base exterior angle
s = 2; length of the two equal sides
sb = 2*s*sin(phi/2); length of base
h = 1; ray entrance height above base max=s*sin(psi)
x = h/cos(phi/2);
t0 = pi/4; ray entrance angle, horizontal=phi/2
t1 = asin(n0*sin(t0)/n1);
t2 = phi-t1;
t3 = asin(n1*sin(t2)/n0);
l0 = (s-x)*sin(phi)/cos(t2);
PRISM : <L(sb) T(a) L(s) Z()>;
CALC : A(n1,n1-0.1) A(t1,asin(n0*sin(t0)/n1)) A(t2,phi-t1)
        A(t3,asin(n1*sin(t2)/n0)) A(l0,(s-x)*sin(phi)/cos(t2));
RAY : [T(t1-pi/2) L(l0) T(t2-t3) L(2)] S(CALC,1);
START : M(0.5) S(PRISM,1) T(psi) M(x) [T(pi/2+t0) L(1)] S(RAY,4);
```

Command line

```
nell prism.nll START 3 | nellsvg 4 2 in 0.02 1 > prism.svg
```

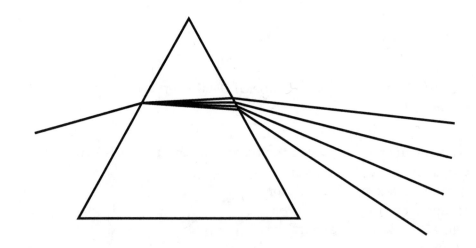

Program (`ball.nll`) Note that lines labeled T1 and `START` are broken
here but are one line each in the actual file.

```
; This shows parallel rays of light being focused by a ball lens
n0 = 1; air index of refraction
n1 = 1.5; lens index of refraction
h = 0.9;
t0 = asin(h);
t1 = asin(n0*h/n1);
T1 : <T(pi/2) M(h) T(-pi/2) L(1.5-sqrt(1-h^2)) T(t1-t0) L(2*cos(t1))
        T(t1-t0) L(sin(2*t1-t0)/sin(2*(t0-t1)))>;
T2 : A(h,h-0.1) A(t0,asin(h)) A(t1,asin(n0*h/n1)) [S(T1,1)];
T3 : A(h,h+0.1) A(t0,asin(h)) A(t1,asin(n0*h/n1)) [S(T1,1)];
START : P(0.25,1) [L(1.5) [T(pi/2) L(1)] C(1) [T(-pi/2) L(1)] L(1.5)]
        S(T2,8) A(h,-0.9) S(T3,8);
```

Command line
```
nell ball.nll START 3 | nellsvg 4 2 in 0.02 1 > ball.svg
```

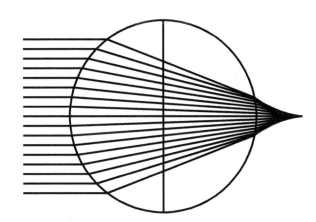

Program (`squarelat.nll`)

```
; Creates a nr x nc square lattice.
; nr = number of rows
; nc = number of columns
; d = lattice spacing
; r = node circle radius
nc = 6;
nr = 6;
d = 1.5;
r = 0.5;
a = pi/2;
T1 : C(r) M(r) L(d-2*r) M(r);
T2 : [S(T1,nc-1) C(r)] T(a) M(d) T(-a);
T3 : M(r) L(d-2*r) M(r);
T4 : [T(a) S(T3,nr-1)] M(d);
PIC : P(0.55,0.55) [S(T2,nr)] S(T4,nc-1) T(a) S(T3,nr-1);
```

Command line

```
nell squarelat.nll PIC 6 | nellsvg 8.6 8.6 cm 0.03 1 > squarelat.svg
```

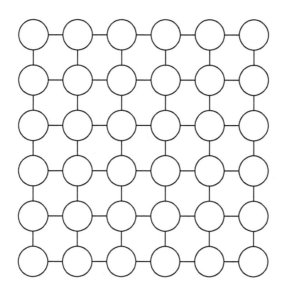

Program (squarepat0.nll)

```
; Creates a simple square tiling.
; d = tile spacing
; d < 1 tiles overlap
; d = 1 exact tiling
; d > 1 tiles space apart
a = pi/2;
d = 1.1;
T1 : L(1) T(a) L(1) T(a) L(1) T(a) L(1) T(a) M(d);
T2 : [S(T1,8)] T(a) M(d) T(-a);
PIC : P(0.15,0.15) S(T2,8);
```

Command line
```
nell squarepat0.nll PIC 6 | nellsvg 9 9 cm 0.03 1 > squarepat0.svg
```

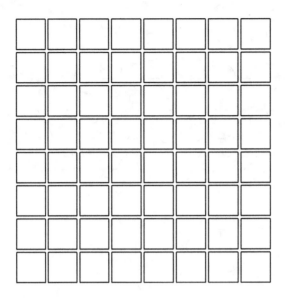

Program (squarepat1.nll)

```
; A square pattern of hexagons, circles and squares.
; d1, d2 = tile spacing
a = pi/2;
b = pi/3;
d1 = 1.5;
d2 = (1+sqrt(3))/2;
n = 4;
A : L(1) T(a) L(1) T(a) L(1) T(a) L(1) T(a);
B : L(1) T(b) L(1) T(b) L(1) T(b) L(1) T(b) L(1) T(b) L(1) T(b);
T2 : C(0.5) T(a/2) M(1/sqrt(2)) T(3*a/2) S(A,1);
T3 : M(1) T(2*b) S(B,1);
T4 : [S(T2,1)] M(d1) [S(T3,1)] M(d1);
T5 : [S(T3,1)] M(d1) [S(T2,1)] M(d1);
T6 : [S(T4,n)] T(a) M(d2) T(-a) [S(T5,n)] T(a) M(d2) T(-a);
PIC : P(1,1) S(T6,n);
```

Command line
```
nell squarepat1.nll PIC 6 | nellsvg 12.5 11.5 cm 0.03 1
  > squarepat1.svg
```

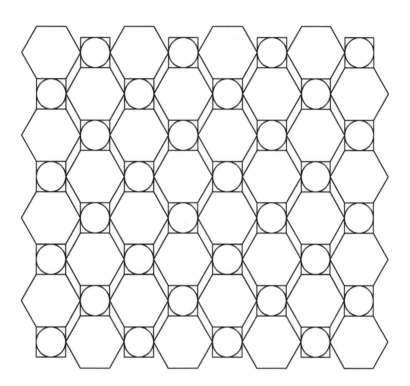

Program (squarepat2.nll)

```
; Creates a square pattern of overlapping hexagons.
; d1, d2 = tile spacing
a = pi/2;
b = pi/3;
d1 = 1.5;
d2 = sqrt(3);
```

```
n = 4;
A : L(1) T(a) L(1) T(a) L(1) T(a) L(1) T(a);
B : L(1) T(b) L(1) T(b) L(1) T(b) L(1) T(b) L(1) T(b) L(1) T(b);
T2 : M(1) T(2*b) S(B,1);
T3 : M(1) T(2*b) S(B,1);
T4 : [S(T2,1)] M(d1) [S(T3,1)] M(d1);
T5 : [S(T3,1)] M(d1) [S(T2,1)] M(d1);
T6 : [S(T4,n)] T(a) M(d2) T(-a) [S(T5,n)] T(a) M(d2) T(-a);
PIC : P(1,1) S(T6,n);
```

Command line

```
nell squarepat2.nll PIC 6 | nellsvg 12.5 14.1 cm 0.03 1 > squarepat2.svg
```

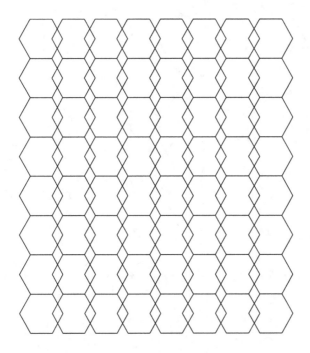

Program (pent0.nll) Note that the line labeled T1 is broken here but is one line in the actual file.

```
; Pentagonal star and pentagram inside pentagon.
a = 2*pi/5;
l = 5;
T1 : A(l,1/2) S(T1,1) A(l,2*l) L(l) T(a) A(l,1/2) S(T1,1) A(l,2*l)
     L(l) T(a) A(l,1/2) S(T1,1) A(l,2*l) L(l) T(a) A(l,1/2) S(T1,1)
     A(l,2*l) L(l) T(a) A(l,1/2) S(T1,1) A(l,2*l) L(l) T(a);
PIC : P(-l/2+4.5,-l/2+3.0) S(T1,1);
```

Command line
```
nell pent0.nll PIC 2 | nellsvg 9 8.5 cm 0.05 1 > pent0.svg
```

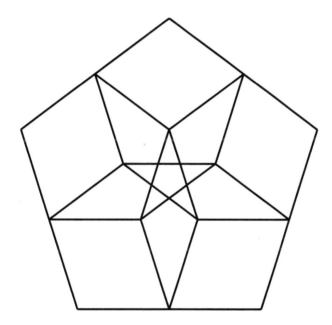

Program (pent1.nll) Note that lines labeled T1, T2 and T3 are broken here but are one line each in the actual file.

```
; Produces a pattern with 31 pentagons.
a = 2*pi/5;
l = 0.5;
T0 : L(l) T(-a) L(l) T(-a) L(l) T(-a) L(l) T(-a) L(l) T(-a);
T1 : S(T2,l) L(l) T(a) S(T2,l) L(l) T(a) S(T2,l) L(l) T(a) S(T2,l)
     L(l) T(a) S(T2,l) L(l) T(a);
T2 : L(l) T(-a) L(l) T(-a) S(T3,l) L(l) T(-a) S(T3,l) L(l) T(-a) L(l)
     T(-a);
T3 : L(l) T(a) L(l) T(a) S(T0,l) L(l) T(a) S(T0,l) L(l) T(a) L(l)
     T(a);
START : P(2.15,2.05) S(T1,l);
```

Command line

```
nell pent1.nll START 4 | nellsvg 4.8 4.6 in 0.02 1 > pent1.svg
```

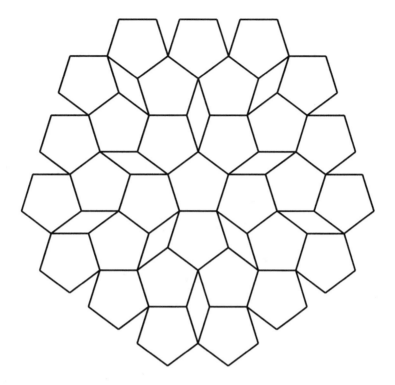

Program (pent2.nll) Note that lines labeled T1, T2, T3 and T4 are broken here but are one line each in the actual file.

```
; Produces a pentagon pattern.
; Size of pattern is controlled by changing the maximum recursion
; level parameter in command line.
a = 2*pi/5;
l = 0.25;
T1 : P(3.7,3.5) S(T2,1) L(l) T(a) S(T2,1) L(l) T(a) S(T2,1) L(l) T(a)
     S(T2,1) L(l) T(a) S(T2,1) L(l) T(a);
T2 : L(l) T(-a) L(l) T(-a) S(T3,1) L(l) T(-a) S(T4,1) L(l) T(-a) L(l)
     T(-a);
```

```
T3 : L(1) T(a) L(1) T(a) L(1) T(-a) L(1) T(-a) S(T3,1) L(1) T(-a)
     S(T4,1) L(1) T(-a) L(1) T(-a) L(1) T(a) L(1) T(-a) L(1) T(-a)
     L(1) T(-a) S(T4,1) L(1) T(-a) L(1) T(-a) L(1) T(a) L(1) T(a);
T4 : L(1) T(a) L(1) T(a) L(1) T(a) L(1) T(-a) L(1) T(-a) L(1) T(-a)
     S(T4,1) L(1) T(-a) L(1) T(-a) L(1) T(a) L(1) T(a);
```

Command line

```
nell pent2.nll T1 6 | nellsvg 7.65 7.25 in 0.02 1 > pent2.svg
```

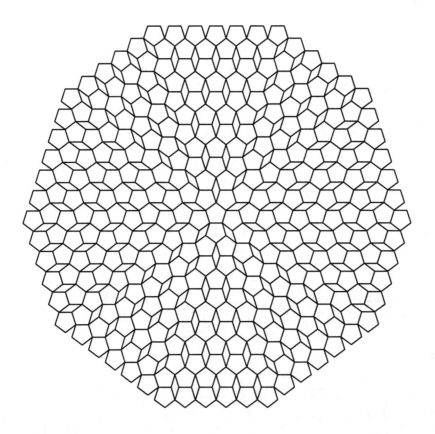

Program (pent3.nll)

```
; Creates a pentagon wreath.
a = 2*pi/5;
r = 1;
s = 0.25;
d = s*(1+sqrt(5))/2;
T0 : <L(s) T(a) L(s) T(a) L(s) T(a) L(s) T(a) Z()>;
T1 : <L(s) T(-a) L(s) T(-a) L(s) T(-a) L(s) T(-a) Z()> M(s) T(a);
T2 : S(T0,1) S(T1,5);
T3 : S(T2,1) T(a/2) M(2*d+s);
START : P(2.65,0.4) S(T3,10);
```

Command line

```
nell pent3.nll START 4 | nellsvg 4.3 4.1 in 0.02 1 > pent3.svg
```

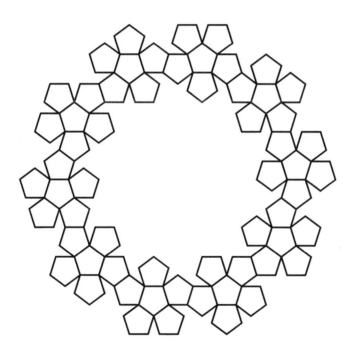

Program (manda01.nll)

```
; A mandala of triangles.
l1 = 8;
l2 = 13;
l3 = 13;
scale = 0.75;
n2 = 5;
a1 = angle(l3,l1,l2);
a2 = angle(l1,l2,l3);
a3 = angle(l2,l3,l1);
dm = l1*sin(a2/2)/(cos(a1/2)*sin(a2/2)+sin(a1/2)*cos(a2/2));
a = 2*pi/n2;
T1 : L(l1) T(pi-a2) L(l2) T(pi-a3) L(l3) T(pi-a1);
PIC1 : S(T1,1) T(a);
PIC3 : [T(a1/2) M(dm) T(-a1/2) S(PIC1,n2)] T(a);
PIC4 : A(l1,scale*l1) A(l2,scale*l2) A(l3,scale*l3) S(PIC3,n2);
PIC5 : P(14,14) S(PIC1,n2) C(l3)  S(PIC4,1);
```

Command line
```
nell manda01.nll PIC5 3 | nellsvg 28 28 mm 0.2 1 > manda01.svg
```

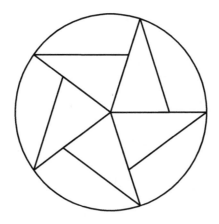

Program (manda03.nll)

```
; A template for creating mandalas with rectangles.
L1 = 13; L1,L2 = sides of rectangle.
L2 = 8; Note: Scaling the same rectangle can make different mandalas.
d = 2;  d = spacing between concentric rectangles
n1 = 1; n1 = number of concentric rectangles
n2 = 10; n2 = number of copies going around the circle
; For scripting, everything below here remains unchanged.
l1 = L1;
l2 = L2;
ai = pi/2;
dm = d*sqrt(2);
a = 2*pi/n2;
T1 : L(l1) T(ai) L(l2) T(ai) L(l1) T(ai) L(l2) T(ai);
PIC2 : S(T1,1) T(ai/2) M(dm) T(-ai/2) A(l1,l1-2*d) A(l2,l2-2*d);
PIC3 : [S(PIC2,n1)] T(a) A(l1,L1) A(l2,L2);
PIC4 : P(20,20) [S(PIC3,n2)] C(sqrt(2)*l1);
```

Command line
```
nell manda03.nll PIC4 10 | nellsvg 40 40 mm 0.2 1 > manda03.svg
```

Program (manda05.nll)

```
; Creates a mandala of equilateral triangles.
a = pi/3;
d = 1.0;
len = 5;
dlen = d/(1.5*tan(a/2));
dm = d/(2*sin(a/2));
T1 : <L(len) T(2*a) L(len) T(2*a) Z()>;
PIC2 : S(T1,1)  A(len,len-dlen) T(a/2) M(dm) T(-a/2);
PIC3 : [S(PIC2,4)] T(a) A(len,5);
PIC4 : P(5,5) [S(PIC3,6)] C(5);
```

Command line

```
nell manda05.nll PIC4 10 | nellsvg 11 11 cm 0.05 1 > manda05.svg
```

Program (`manda07.nll`) Note that lines labeled `circ` and `PIC2` are broken here but are one line each in the actual file.

```
; A mandala of triangles with the largest inscribed circle
; inside each triangle.
L1 = 10;
L2 = 10;
L3 = 10;
d = 2;
n1 = 2;
n2 = 5;
l1 = L1;
l2 = L2;
l3 = L3;
a1 = angle(l3,l1,l2);
```

```
a2 = angle(l1,l2,l3);
a3 = angle(l2,l3,l1);
d1 = d/tan(a1/2);
d2 = d/tan(a2/2);
d3 = d/tan(a3/2);
dm = d/sin(a1/2);
cm = sin(a2/2)/(cos(a1/2)*sin(a2/2)+sin(a1/2)*cos(a2/2));
a = 2*pi/n2;
tri : L(l1) T(pi-a2) L(l2) T(pi-a3) L(l3) T(pi-a1);
circ : T(a1/2) M(l1*cm) C(sqrt((-l1+l2+l3)*(l1-l2+l3)*(l1+l2-l3)/
       (l1+l2+l3))/2) T(-a1/2);
PIC2 : S(tri,1) [S(circ,1)] T(a1/2) M(dm) T(-a1/2) A(l1,l1-d1-d2)
       A(l2,l2-d2-d3) A(l3,l3-d1-d3);
PIC3 : [S(PIC2,n1)] T(a) A(l1,L1) A(l2,L2) A(l3,L3);
PIC4 : P(l1,l1) [S(PIC3,n2)] C(L3);
```

Command line

```
nell manda07.nll PIC4 3 | nellsvg 22 22 mm 0.2 1 > manda07.svg
```

Program (manda09.nll) Note that lines labeled S1 and PIC2 are broken
here but are one line each in the actual file.

```
; A template for creating mandalas with triangles.
L1 = 10; L1,L2,L3 = sides of triangles.
L2 = 10; Note: Scaling the same triangle can make different mandalas.
L3 = 10;
d = 2;  d = spacing between concentric triangles
n1 = 1; n1 = number of concentric triangles
n2 = 6; n2 = number of copies going around the circle
l1 = L1;
l2 = L2;
l3 = L3;
a1 = pi/3;
d1 = d/tan(a1/2);
dm = d/sin(a1/2);
a = 2*pi/n2;
T1 : L(l1) T(pi-a1) S(S1,1) L(l2) T(pi-a1) L(l3) T(pi-a1);
S1 : L(l2) T(-pi/2) L(l2) T(-pi/2) S(T1,1) L(l2) T(-pi/2) L(l2)
     T(-pi/2);
PIC2 : S(T1,1) T(a1/2) M(dm) T(-a1/2) A(l1,l1-2*d1) A(l2,l2-2*d1)
       A(l3,l3-2*d1);
PIC3 : [S(PIC2,n1)] T(a) A(l1,L1) A(l2,L2) A(l3,L3);
PIC4 : P(40,40) [S(PIC3,n2)];
```

Command line
```
nell manda09.nll PIC4 9 | nellsvg 80 80 mm 0.2 1 > manda09.svg
```

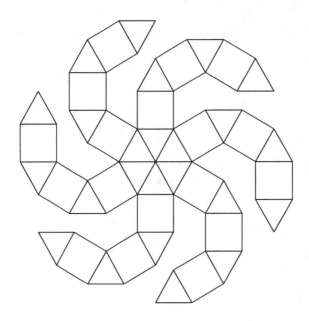

Program (manda11.nll) Note that lines labeled T1, S1, PIC2 and PIC4 are broken here but are one line each in the actual file.

```
; A template for creating mandalas with triangles.
L1 = 10; L1,L2,L3 = sides of triangles.
L2 = 10; Note: Scaling the same triangle can make different mandalas.
L3 = 10;
d = 2; d = spacing between concentric triangles
n1 = 1; n1 = number of concentric triangles
n2 = 1; n2 = number of copies going around the circle
l1 = L1;
l2 = L2;
l3 = L3;
a1 = pi/3;
d1 = d/tan(a1/2);
dm = d/sin(a1/2);
```

```
a = 2*pi/n2;
T1 : L(l1) T(pi-a1) S(S1,1) L(l2) T(pi-a1) S(S1,1) L(l3) T(pi-a1)
     S(S1,1);
S1 : L(l2) T(-pi/2) L(l2) T(-pi/2) S(T1,1) L(l2) T(-pi/2) L(l2)
     T(-pi/2);
PIC2 : S(T1,1) T(a1/2) M(dm) T(-a1/2) A(l1,l1-2*d1) A(l2,l2-2*d1)
       A(l3,l3-2*d1);
PIC3 : [S(PIC2,n1)] T(a) A(l1,L1) A(l2,L2) A(l3,L3);
PIC4 : P(62,65) [S(PIC3,n2)] T(a1/2) M(l1/(2*cos(a1/2))) T(-a1/2)
       C(60.0) C(65.0);
```

Command line

```
nell manda11.nll PIC4 11 | nellsvg 135 135 mm 0.2 1 > manda11.svg
```

Program (manda13.nll)


```
; Has intertwined production rules (T1 and T2), and produces
; a mandala of triangles, where the most important parameter is the
; maximum substitution level, given on the command line, with a
; higher number making longer mandala arms.
n2 = 10;
a = 2*pi/n2;
l1 = 8;
l2 = 13;
l3 = 13;
k1 = 5;
k2 = 8;
k3 = 8;
a1 = angle(l3,l1,l2);
a2 = angle(l1,l2,l3);
a3 = angle(l2,l3,l1);
b1 = angle(k3,k1,k2);
b2 = angle(k1,k2,k3);
b3 = angle(k2,k3,k1);
T1 : L(l1) T(pi-a2) S(T2,1) L(l2) T(pi-a3) L(l3) T(pi-a1);
T2 : L(k1) T(b2-pi) S(T1,1) L(k2) T(b3-pi) L(k3) T(b1-pi);
PIC1 : [S(T1,1)] T(a);
PIC2 : P(32,32) S(PIC1,n2);
```


Command line
```
nell manda13.nll PIC2 7 | nellsvg 65 65 mm 0.2 1 > manda13.svg
```

Program (manda15.nll) Note that the line labeled ALL is broken here but is one line in the actual file.

```
; Creates a mandala with pentagonal symmetry.
a = 2*pi/5;
b1 = pi - angle(3, 10, 12);
b2 = pi - angle(10, 12, 3);
b3 = pi - angle(12, 3, 10);
c1 = pi - angle(3, 8, 10);
c2 = pi - angle(8, 10, 3);
c3 = pi - angle(10, 3, 8);
d1 = pi - angle(3, 6, 8);
d2 = pi - angle(6, 8, 3);
d3 = pi - angle(8, 3, 6);
e1 = pi - angle(3, 4, 6);
```

```
e2 = pi - angle(4, 6, 3);
e3 = pi - angle(6, 3, 4);
f1 = pi - angle(3, 2, 4);
f2 = pi - angle(2, 4, 3);
f3 = pi - angle(4, 3, 2);
stem = 3.9; stem defines the distance btw the lobes of the mandala
r = 0.5; r is a scale factor
R1 : T(-b3) L(r*3) T(-b1) [S(R2,1)] L(r*10);
R2 : T(pi-c3) L(r*3) T(-c1) [S(R3,1)] L(r*8);
R3 : T(pi-d3) L(r*3) T(-d1) [S(R4,1)] L(r*6);
R4 : T(pi-e3) L(r*3) T(-e1) [S(R5,1)] L(r*4);
R5 : T(pi-f3) L(r*3) T(-f1) L(r*2);
L1 : T(b3) L(r*3) T(b1) [S(L2,1)] L(r*10);
L2 : T(c3-pi) L(r*3) T(c1) [S(L3,1)] L(r*8);
L3 : T(d3-pi) L(r*3) T(d1) [S(L4,1)] L(r*6);
L4 : T(e3-pi) L(r*3) T(e1) [S(L5,1)] L(r*4);
L5 : T(f3-pi) L(r*3) T(f1) L(r*2);
LEAF: L(r*12) [S(R1,1)] [S(L1,1)];
ALL: P(8,6.5) T(a/4) [L(r*stem) S(LEAF,1)] T(a) [L(r*stem) S(LEAF,1)]
     T(a) [L(r*stem) S(LEAF,1)] T(a) [L(r*stem) S(LEAF,1)] T(a)
     [L(r*stem) S(LEAF,1)];
```

Command line
```
nell manda15.nll ALL 10 | nellsvg 16 14.5 cm 0.05 1 > manda15.svg
```

Program (manda17.nll) Note that lines labeled CORNERTR and CIRCLES are broken here but are one line each in the actual file.

```
; Creates a mandala of square symmetry.
a = 2*pi/5;
b1 = pi - angle(3, 10, 12);
b2 = pi - angle(10, 12, 3);
b3 = pi - angle(12, 3, 10);
```

```
c1 = pi - angle(3, 8, 10);
c2 = pi - angle(8, 10, 3);
c3 = pi - angle(10, 3, 8);
d1 = pi - angle(3, 6, 8);
d2 = pi - angle(6, 8, 3);
d3 = pi - angle(8, 3, 6);
e1 = pi - angle(3, 4, 6);
e2 = pi - angle(4, 6, 3);
e3 = pi - angle(6, 3, 4);
f1 = pi - angle(3, 2, 4);
f2 = pi - angle(2, 4, 3);
f3 = pi - angle(4, 3, 2);
stem = 3.9; stem defines the distance btw the lobes of the mandala
r = 0.25; scale factor
R1 : T(-b3) L(r*3) T(-b1) [S(R2,1)] L(r*10);
R2 : T(pi-c3) L(r*3) T(-c1) [S(R3,1)] L(r*8);
R3 : T(pi-d3) L(r*3) T(-d1) [S(R4,1)] L(r*6);
R4 : T(pi-e3) L(r*3) T(-e1) [S(R5,1)] L(r*4);
R5 : T(pi-f3) L(r*3) T(-f1) L(r*2);
L1 : T(b3) L(r*3) T(b1) [S(L2,1)] L(r*10);
L2 : T(c3-pi) L(r*3) T(c1) [S(L3,1)] L(r*8);
L3 : T(d3-pi) L(r*3) T(d1) [S(L4,1)] L(r*6);
L4 : T(e3-pi) L(r*3) T(e1) [S(L5,1)] L(r*4);
L5 : T(f3-pi) L(r*3) T(f1) L(r*2);
CORNERBL : P(1,1) [L(r*12) S(R1,1)] [T(pi/2) L(r*12) S(L1,1)];
CORNERBR : P(10,1) [T(pi) L(r*12) S(L1,1)] [T(pi/2) L(r*12) S(R1,1)];
CORNERTL : P(1,10) [T(-pi/2) L(r*12) S(R1,1)] [T(0) L(r*12) S(L1,1)];
CORNERTR : P(10,10) [T(pi) L(r*12) S(R1,1)] [T(-pi/2) L(r*12)
            S(L1,1)];
SQUARE : S(CORNERBL,1) S(CORNERBR,1) S(CORNERTL,1) S(CORNERTR,1);
CENTRAL : T(pi/2) [S(R1,1)] [S(L1,1)];
CIRCLES : P(5.5,5.5) C(r*1) C(r*19) P(r*9+5.5,5.5) C(r*2)
```

```
         P(r*-9+5.5,5.5) C(r*2) P(5.5,r*9+5.5) C(r*2) P(5.5,r*-9+5.5)
         C(r*2) P(5.5,r*16+5.5) C(r*3) P(5.5,r*-16+5.5) C(r*3)
         P(r*16+5.5,5.5) C(r*3) P(r*-16+5.5,5.5) C(r*3);
TOTAL : P(5.5,5.5) [S(SQUARE,1)] [T(pi/4) S(CENTRAL,4)] S(CIRCLES,1);
```

Command line

```
nell manda17.nll TOTAL 10 | nellsvg 11 11 cm 0.05 1 > manda17.svg
```

Program (manda19.nll) Note that the line labeled PIC2 is broken here but is one line in the actual file.


```
; A template for creating mandalas with triangles.
L1 = 10; L1,L2,L3 = sides of triangles.
L2 = 10; Note: Scaling the same triangle can make different mandalas.
L3 = 10;
d = 2.5; d = spacing between concentric triangles
n1 = 4; n1 = number of concentric triangles
n2 = 6; n2 = number of copies going around the circle
l1 = L1;
l2 = L2;
l3 = L3;
a1 = angle(l3,l1,l2);
a2 = angle(l1,l2,l3);
a3 = angle(l2,l3,l1);
d1 = d/tan(a1/2);
d2 = d/tan(a2/2);
d3 = d/tan(a3/2);
dm = d/sin(a1/2);
a = 2*pi/n2;
T1 : L(l1) T(pi-a2) L(l2) T(pi-a3) L(l3) T(pi-a1);
PIC2 : S(T1,1) T(a1/2) M(dm) T(-a1/2) A(l1,l1-d1-d2) A(l2,l2-d2-d3)
       A(l3,l3-d1-d3);
PIC3 : [S(PIC2,n1)] T(a) A(l1,L1) A(l2,L2) A(l3,L3);
PIC4 : P(15,15) [S(PIC3,n2)] C(L3) C(1.5*L3);
```


Command line
```
nell manda19.nll PIC4 10 | nellsvg 30 30 mm 0.1 1 > manda19.svg
```

Program (lonestar.nll)

```
; Produces a star-like figure using paralelograms.
; d = tile spacing
; d < 1 tiles overlap
; d = 1 exact tiling
; d > 1 tiles space apart
a = pi/4;
l = 0.4;
d = 1.25*l;
n = 4;
T1 : L(l) T(a) L(l) T(3*a) L(l) T(a) L(l) T(3*a) M(d);
T2 : [S(T1,n)] T(a) M(d) T(-a);
```

```
T3 : [S(T2,n)] T(a);
T4 : P(3.25,3.25) S(T3,8);
```

Command line

```
nell lonestar.nll T4 10 | nellsvg 6.5 6.5 in 0.02 1 > lonestar.svg
```

Program (cross.nll)

```
; Creates a cross with an octagon at center.
s = 1; "s" makes tips longer with increase.
r = s; "r" makes junction side wider with increase.
a = 2*pi/5; "a" makes tips more pointy with increase.
t1 = 3*s; "t1" makes 3 arms longer with increase.
; b1 is angle of side near junction.
b1 = acos((s/t1)*cos(a/2)-r/(2*t1));
c1 = pi-a/2-b1; "c1" is angle of side near point
t2 = 5*s; t2,b2,c2 are long arm versions of t1,b1,c1
b2 = acos((s/t2)*cos(a/2)-r/(2*t2));
c2 = pi-a/2-b2;
; T1 is the 3 short arms, T2 is longer arm.
T1 : L(r) T(-b1) L(t1) T(-c1) L(s) T(-a) L(s) T(-c1) L(t1) T(-b1);
T2 : L(r) T(-b2) L(t2) T(-c2) L(s) T(-a) L(s) T(-c2) L(t2) T(-b2);
T3 : L(s) T(pi/4); T3 is a side of octagon
T4 : S(T3,8); T4 is octagon at junction
; T5 makes longer arm, T6 makes shorter arms.
T5 : M((s-r)/2) S(T2,1) M((s+r)/2) T(pi/4) M(s) T(pi/4);
T6 : M((s-r)/2) S(T1,1) M((s+r)/2) T(pi/4) M(s) T(pi/4);
PIC : P(4.5,5.8) S(T4,1) S(T5,1) S(T6,3);
```

Command line
```
nell cross.nll PIC 6 | nellsvg 10 12 cm 0.05 1 > cross.svg
```

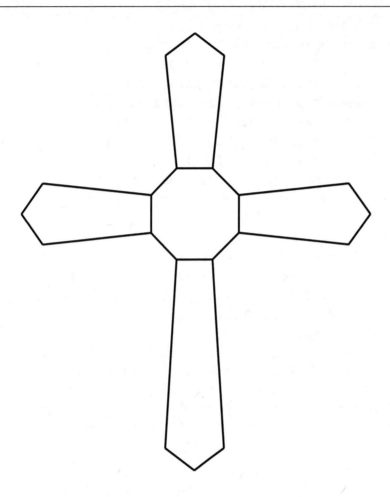

USEFUL IDENTITIES

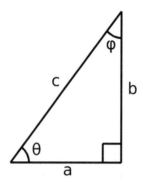

For the right triangle shown above the following identities hold.

Pythagorean identity.

$$a^2 + b^2 = c^2 \qquad (1)$$

Sum of internal angles.

$$\theta + \phi = \frac{\pi}{2} \qquad (2)$$

Trigonometric identities.

$$\cos\theta = \frac{a}{c} \qquad (3)$$

$$\sin\theta = \frac{b}{c} \qquad (4)$$

$$\tan\theta = \frac{b}{a} \qquad (5)$$

$$\cos\phi = \sin\theta \tag{6}$$

$$\sin\phi = \cos\theta \tag{7}$$

$$\tan\phi = \frac{1}{\tan\theta} \tag{8}$$

General trigonometric identities.

$$\cos(-\phi) = \cos\phi \tag{9}$$

$$\sin(-\phi) = -\sin\phi \tag{10}$$

$$\tan(-\phi) = -\tan\phi \tag{11}$$

$$\cos(\theta \pm \phi) = \cos\theta\cos\phi \mp \sin\theta\sin\phi \tag{12}$$

$$\sin(\theta \pm \phi) = \sin\theta\cos\phi \pm \cos\theta\sin\phi \tag{13}$$

$$\tan(\theta \pm \phi) = \frac{\tan\theta \pm \tan\phi}{1 \mp \tan\theta\tan\phi} \tag{14}$$

$$\cos 2\theta = \cos^2\theta - \sin^2\theta \tag{15}$$

$$\sin 2\theta = 2\sin\theta\cos\theta \tag{16}$$

$$\tan 2\theta = \frac{2\tan\theta}{1 - \tan^2\theta} \tag{17}$$

$$\cos\left(\theta \pm \pi\right) = -\cos\theta \tag{18}$$

$$\sin\left(\theta \pm \pi\right) = -\sin\theta \tag{19}$$

$$\cos\left(\theta \pm \pi/2\right) = \mp\sin\theta \tag{20}$$

$$\sin\left(\theta \pm \pi/2\right) = \pm\cos\theta \tag{21}$$

$$\cos\left(\theta \pm \pi/3\right) = \frac{\cos\theta \mp \sqrt{3}\sin\theta}{2} \tag{22}$$

$$\sin\left(\theta \pm \pi/3\right) = \frac{\sin\theta \pm \sqrt{3}\cos\theta}{2} \tag{23}$$

$$\cos\left(\theta \pm \pi/4\right) = \frac{\cos\theta \mp \sin\theta}{\sqrt{2}} \tag{24}$$

$$\sin\left(\theta \pm \pi/4\right) = \frac{\sin\theta \pm \cos\theta}{\sqrt{2}} \tag{25}$$

$$\cos\theta\cos\phi = \frac{1}{2}\left[\cos\left(\theta - \phi\right) + \cos\left(\theta + \phi\right)\right] \tag{26}$$

$$\sin\theta\sin\phi = \frac{1}{2}\left[\cos\left(\theta - \phi\right) - \cos\left(\theta + \phi\right)\right] \tag{27}$$

$$\sin\theta\cos\phi = \frac{1}{2}\left[\sin\left(\theta - \phi\right) + \sin\left(\theta + \phi\right)\right] \tag{28}$$

$$A\cos\theta + B\sin\theta = \sqrt{A^2 + B^2}\cos\left(\theta - \phi\right) \tag{29}$$

$$\phi = \tan^{-1}\left(B/A\right) \tag{30}$$

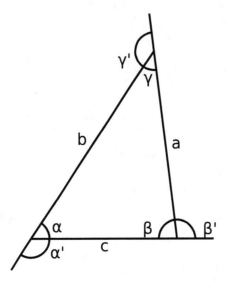

For the general triangle shown above the following identities hold.

Sum of internal angles.

$$\alpha + \beta + \gamma = \pi \tag{31}$$

Sum of external angles.

$$\alpha' + \beta' + \gamma' = 2\pi \tag{32}$$

External angle as sum of opposite internal angles.

$$\alpha' = \beta + \gamma \tag{33}$$
$$\beta' = \alpha + \gamma \tag{34}$$
$$\gamma' = \alpha + \beta \tag{35}$$

Law of cosines.

$$a^2 = b^2 + c^2 - 2bc\cos\alpha \tag{36}$$
$$b^2 = a^2 + c^2 - 2ac\cos\beta \tag{37}$$
$$c^2 = a^2 + b^2 - 2ab\cos\gamma \tag{38}$$

Law of sines.

$$\frac{\sin\alpha}{a} = \frac{\sin\beta}{b} = \frac{\sin\gamma}{c} \tag{39}$$

ACKNOWLEDGMENTS

In ordinary life we hardly realize that we receive a great deal more than we give, and that it is only with gratitude that life becomes rich. It is very easy to overestimate the importance of our own achievements in comparison with what we owe to others.

   Dietrich Bonhoeffer, letter to parents from prison, Sept. 13, 1943

We'd like to thank our parents, Istvan and Anna Hollos, for helping us in many ways.

We thank the makers and maintainers of all the software we've used in the production of this book, including: gcc, Emacs text editor, LaTeX typesetting system, Inkscape, ImageMagick, mupdf and evince document viewers, bash shell, and the GNU/Linux operating system.

ABOUT THE AUTHORS

Stefan Hollos and **J. Richard Hollos** are physicists and electrical engineers by training, and enjoy anything related to math, physics, engineering and computing. In addition, they enjoy creating music and visual art, and being in the great outdoors. They are the authors of:

- **Coin Tossing: The Hydrogen Atom of Probability**

- **Creating Melodies**

- **Hexagonal Tilings and Patterns**

- **Combinatorics II Problems and Solutions: Counting Patterns**

- **Information Theory: A Concise Introduction**

- **Recursive Digital Filters: A Concise Guide**

- **Art of Pi**

- **Creating Noise**

- **Art of the Golden Ratio**

- **Creating Rhythms**

- **Pattern Generation for Computational Art**

- **Finite Automata and Regular Expressions: Problems and Solutions**

- **Probability Problems and Solutions**

- **Combinatorics Problems and Solutions**

- **The Coin Toss: Probabilities and Patterns**

- **Pairs Trading: A Bayesian Example**

- **Simple Trading Strategies That Work**

- **Bet Smart: The Kelly System for Gambling and Investing**

- **Signals from the Subatomic World: How to Build a Proton Precession Magnetometer**

They are brothers and business partners at Exstrom Laboratories LLC in Longmont, Colorado. Their website is exstrom.com

THANK YOU

Thank you for buying this book.

If you'd like to receive news about this book and others published by Abrazol Publishing, just go to

http://www.abrazol.com/

and sign up for our newsletter.